C000274286

The Illustrated
History of
Architecture

The Illustrated History of
Architecture

THE DEVELOPMENT
OF CITIES AND TOWNS

By Benjamin Fragner

SUNBURST BOOKS

Text by Benjamin Fragner
Illustrations by Michal Brix and Eva Smrčinová
Translated by Alena Linhartová
Graphic design by Miroslav Němec

Designed and produced by Aventinum
English language edition first published 1994 by
Sunburst Books, 65 Old Church Street, London SW3 5BS

©Aventinum, Prague 1994

All rights reserved. No part of this publication may be
reproduced, stored in a retrieval system, or transmitted,
in any form or by any means, electronic, mechanical,
photocopying, recording or otherwise, without the prior
permission of the copyright holder.

ISBN 1 85778 040 X

Printed in the Czech Republic by Polygrafia, Prague
1/22/11/51-01

Contents

I *A Gateway into Times Gone By*

The First Cities

A tower 8.5 metres high with a staircase rises from the bottom of one of the excavated trenches. The story of the earliest cities begins on this small plot of excavated earth in Ariba, a town with an Arab name, situated a mere twenty kilometres from the Dead Sea in the present-day Jordan.

On the outskirts of Ariba there was a small mound (a tell), one of many located there. It contained the remains of previous habitats, piled one on top of another; new dwellings rising from the ruins of their ancestors' housing and middens. Over the course of centuries these successive layers have created an elevated place in the countryside. This mound bears the name Tell-el-Sultan, the Sultan's Mound.

And it was here that Kathleen Kenyon, an English archaeologist, made the discovery which clarified speculations concerning the first town settlements on Earth. She found the remains of a town which, to the surprise of many archaeologists, was even older than any of the ancient cities of Mesopotamia. It was, therefore, necessary to shift the origins of history several thousand years forward and to alter names and dates. We touch history there, on that very archaeological site, amongst the mounds of soil and stone, next to the foundations of excavated buildings, the motionless reminders of bygone times.

Kathleen Kenyon was, in

Looking at the undulating terrain stretching ahead of us, we can almost envisage the foundations of early dwellings. The remains of the earliest town on Earth are hidden deep underneath masses of soil at a site situated between a green oasis and the outskirts of modern Jericho.

The Biblical story about the destruction of Jericho depicted on a wood engraving in what is known as the Melantrich Bible dating from the 16th century. In fact, the picture does not present Jericho as is really looked in its heyday but provides a fictional depiction of a depraved, sinful human settlement, reflecting contemporary views when the engraving was made. It illustrates the words from the Book of Joshua, which voiced many of the criticisms of and objections to the great human settlements which were frequently raised in later centuries—as shown in the following chapters: 'And the city shall be accursed, *even* it and all that *are* therein . . .'. That was the reason why its inhabitants were punished, as mentioned several lines later: 'And they burnt the city with fire, and all that was therein . . .'. In fact, Kathleen Kenyon was searching for the very ruins of Jericho under mounds of earth.

fact, searching for the remains of the Biblical town of Jericho. Its tragic fortunes described in the Old Testament (Joshua, Chapter Six) have excited and inspired many historians and writers. After extensive excavation work conducted between 1952 and 1958 on the Sultan's Mound, she discovered in the trench the remains of much older town walls than she had expected. The Jericho which she discovered was already founded in the 8th or even at the beginning of the 9th millennium B.C. by Neolithic peoples. The tower with its staircase was probably situated in the town centre and served a defensive purpose or was possibly a religious symbol. The settlement was surrounded by a thick wall made of small chiselled stones and a defensive eight metre wide and two metre deep moat. According to one estimate, Jericho had about three thousand inhabitants in the 8th millennium B.C. Such a large number of people seems to provide evidence that this place was not merely an agricultural settlement but a predecessor of future towns.

Why did people gather in such numbers in that particular place? Why did they decide to settle there and erect buildings whose foundations have survived until the present day?

The latest excavations seem to confirm that the first settled agrarian people discovered, collected and cultivated wild plants such as wheat, barley, peas and lentils in this region of the Middle East — on the

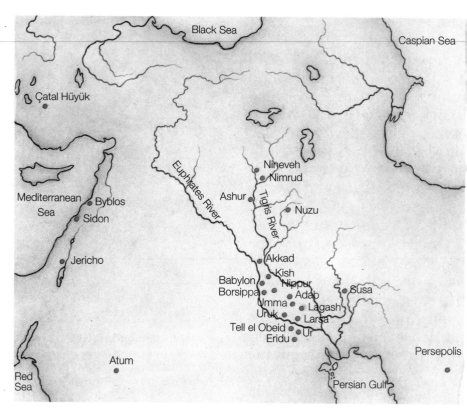

The region of the earliest urban civilizations. The greatest growth of cities took place in the basin of the Euphrates and the Tigris in Mesopotamia.

hillsides of Palestine and Syria; at the foot of the mountains on the Iran-Iraq border; and on the mountain plateaux of Anatolia. These areas were and still are the natural habitat of many animals which man has domesticated. This abundance of agricultural resources is the main reason why the first towns on Earth appeared just there. The more advanced agriculture provided food for a greater number of people, not just those who were directly involved in producing it.

The people of Jericho made their living from growing wheat and barley. However, the development of the town was also influenced by its highly favourable position

close to sources of water in an oasis and on a route to the deposits of salt, sulphur and bitumen near the Dead Sea. The oasis was the crossroads of routes leading to Southern Palestine and Anatolia and the routes connecting nomad desert camps and the Mediterranean.

Soon after the discovery of Jericho, in 1961 an archaeologist called James Mellaart excavated another Neolithic settlement which can also be considered a precursor of present day towns. It is situated on the Anatolian plain forty kilometres from the Turkish town of Konya. It provides a further episode in the slowly emerging story of human habitation.

Its original name is not

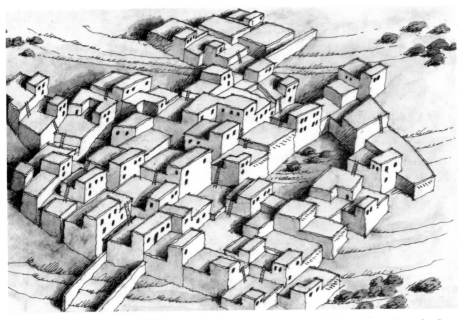

An unusual town without streets. Human dwellings made of clay bricks, with houses clustered together like a honeycomb. The daylight penetrated the houses through small windows in the upper part of the walls. It seems likely that, in absence of roads, access to neighbouring houses was along flat roofs connected by ladders. This is a modern view of Çatal Hüyük based on James Mellaart's excavations.

During his excavation work Mellaart discovered the remains of a mysterious ceremonial chamber and named it the Temple of the Bull God. The early inhabitants of this town could only gain access to it by using a ladder lowered through a hole in the roof.

known, so it was named Çatal Hüyük, meaning 'dual mound', because of the elevation created by its heaped ruins. This settlement was founded later than Jericho as its origins date from the period 6500—5700 B.C. It was, however, larger and its inhabitants were more sophisticated. Its area of twelve and a half hectares could provide accommodation for up to ten thousand inhabitants. Archaeologists have gathered much information about their lives. The settlers were experienced agrarian people who kept in their houses special storage places for wheat, barley, millet, peas and lentils, which they cultivated. They pressed oil from pistachio nuts and almonds. They were also skilled artisans who produced weapons and jewellery from copper and lead; they carved, engraved and polished statues from wood, stone and bones and they used jars and tiny spoons and forks for cosmetic purposes. The development of this settlement was undoubtedly influenced by nearby deposits of obsidian, a dark volcanic rock resembling bottle glass, which was the primary material for the production of various tools and ornaments by Neolithic people.

Çatal Hüyük was abandoned after about eight hundred years, presenting us with another mystery.

Why was this town deserted? There are no ready answers to this question yet, just guesses and conjectures. Archaeologists have not yet discovered a simple answer explaining this sudden change in the fortunes of the thousands of inhabitants. Perhaps an enemy attack, the spread of a contagious disease, a fire or another natural disaster struck suddenly. These were the most common causes leading to the extinction of flourishing towns in the past. However, it is also possible that the town itself lost the reason for its existence, when traders and artisans no longer needed the obsidian which had made this settlement rich and prosperous. Or did the exhausted fields nearby stop yielding enough agricultural produce and crops to feed large numbers of people?

Mesopotamian Cities

Urban settlements in the fertile region between the Rivers

The earliest written and pictorial records provide us with an insight into the Sumerian theory of the arrangement of space, which presented the Earth as a loaf of bread floating on the ocean of the universe. It was surrounded by a mighty wall, a type of town fortification, which prevented flooding by the ocean waves. This Sumerian theory was influenced by their knowledge of town building.

From the earliest times, the most fearsome danger to threaten the security of towns was war. This alabaster relief discovered in Nineveh, one of the earliest cities, pillaging the Elamite town of Haman.

Tigris and Euphrates, part of present-day Iraq, might correspond better to our modern notion of towns. Babylon, the first metropolis, was established in this region.

Babylon was not the first large city, but it represents a turning point, as the development of urban civilization reached a level here which was later to be copied elsewhere in the world.

The alluvial plain in the basin of the rivers was the most suitable place for settlement to occur. It provided abundant cereal crops, vegetables and spices. It was on the crossroads to the Arabian Peninsula as well as the Iranian and Iraqi mountains; a silver and gold trade route to Asia Minor passed through this region. The rivers were used to transport valuable cypress and cedar timber to the Mediterranean. In the 4th millennium

B.C., the Sumerians settled there and their civilization made a significant contribution to the foundation of the first city states. Upstream on the rivers were the towns of Eridu, Uruk, Lagash, Shuruppak, Umma, Nippur, Kish.... Why did these towns appear in this particular region? In order to feed an ever growing population, it was necessary to increase food production by building an extensive network of irrigation canals. This was a task which could only be achieved by a community of people equipped with tools, construction materials and the necessary knowledge and skills. It was safer and more comfortable to live within an enclosed town, although there were restrictive rules and obligations.

A small tablet, 21 × 8 cm, seems to be the earliest preserved town plan. It was discovered together with other cuneiform tablets in a clay vase excavated at Nippur. Around 1500 B.C. a Sumerian cartographer depicted the arrangement of an early Sumerian cultural centre with all the important buildings and temples; the central park; the river and canals; town walls and gates.

The development of human habitats is depicted in various objects dating back to ancient times. One example is a cast bronze panel, probably a wall decoration, 2,500 years old, from Urartu, which was situated on a fertile plateau in Asia Minor. It provides remarkable evidence of the shape of a fortified building with a gate, windows and battlements. In addition, it provides us with information about the town's economic life, and about the local craftsmen who mastered working with bronze. The people of this area took advantage of the rich copper mines in nearby Lesser Caucasia to develop a lucrative trade in bronze products, selling them even as far afield as Greece and in the Etruscan cities.

Archaeologists have excavated the remains of Sumerian towns and found clay tablets written in a cuneiform script which is the earliest script known to exist.

The Sumerian script was established in the 4th millennium B.C. as a result of the cultural and economic aspirations of the city states. Other nations which later contributed to the political and economic development of Mesopotamia, namely the Semite Akkadian-Babylonians, the Assyrians, the Elamites, the Amorites and the Kassites, continued this written tradition. We are, therefore, not left only with excavated foundations and fortifications, or scattered broken pottery of domestic utensils. Written documents allow us an insight into the inhabitants' thinking, their way of life and relationships to their towns.

One of the clay tablets, which was discovered in a library or rather in a heap of similar tablets at Nineveh, contains a ballad about Etan, a hero of Mesopotamian legends. It also briefly summarizes considerations about towns: 'Let the town be a nesting place, a settlement of people.'

Towns with a layout of crooked, narrow streets were rebuilt into imposing and carefully planned metropolies in the Middle East.

A family house in a Mesopotamian town was designed around a central courtyard from which access was provided to individual rooms, divided into a private dwelling part and a commercial or farming area. Houses were often onestorey buildings, with sanitary amenities.

Babylon became the most grandiose metropolis. Despite the fact that it had been completely destroyed several times, Nebuchadnezzar II, son of Nabopolassar who founded the Neo-Babylonian Empire, rebuilt Babylon into a rich and mighty city in the years 604—539 B.C. Nebuchadnezzar also had a famous tower built, 'the House of the Heaven and Earth's foundations', which was a ninety metre tall pyramidal ziggurat with stages surmounted by a temple of Marduk, God of Babylon. The King invited the best scientists and artisans to Babylon. They built technically demanding structures; created monumental statues and painted magnificent murals; wrote works of literature and studied the stars. They succeeded in calculating and measuring time precisely and in healing dangerous diseases.

The Babylonians wrote several cuneiform guides to the city on clay tablets, which were undoubtedly the first tourist guides in history. By comparing these guides and information provided by later travellers to the city with the results of archaeological excavations, it has been established that Babylon in the 6th

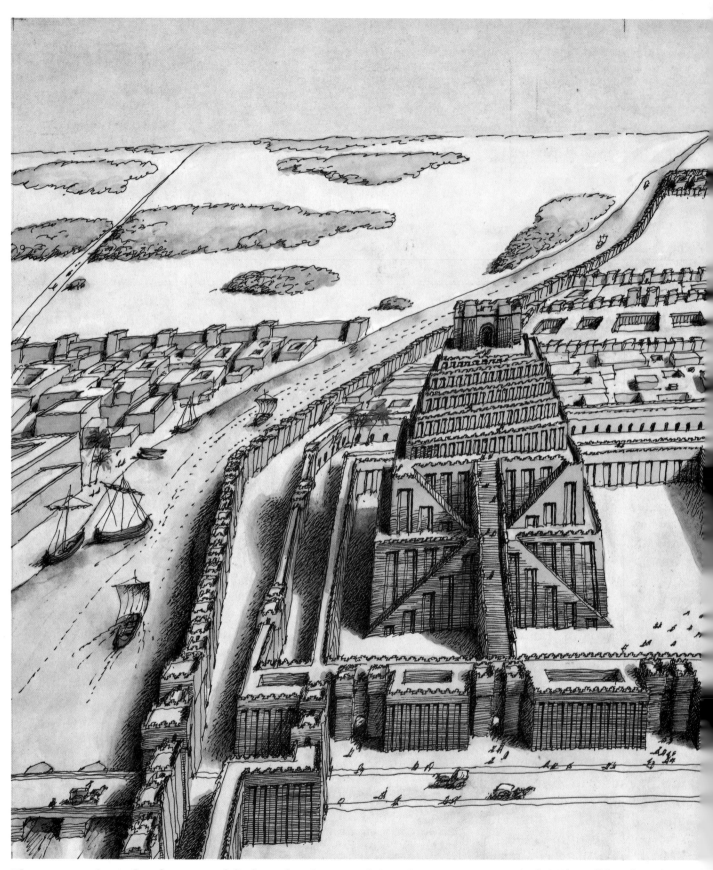

The systematic study of excavated finds and written records which provide us with an insight into the daily life and imposing layout of Babylon has been going on for nearly one hundred years. The Babylon of the 6th century B.C. was dominated by the Tower of Babel; its left side was enclosed by the town walls and the River Euphrates, beyond which a new town was gradually spreading. To the right of the Tower,

century B.C. covered an area of ten square kilometres. The city was protected by a water moat and three rings of walls. The earlier eastern part of the city was connected with the newer western part by a 123 metre long bridge, a unique achievement of the builder's craft. Thus, Babylon was not only famous for its Tower, the forerunner of subsequent high-rise structures.

The twenty-four metre wide Marduk's Avenue used for processions was also legendary. It was enclosed on both sides by a high wall decorated with a coloured ceramic frieze three hundred metres long. This wall centred the attention of visitors on one point like a magnifying glass focusing the sun's rays into one spot. This wall in Babylon was an example of a well-planned urban architecture which was able to evoke strong emotional feelings and simultaneously contributed to the town defence. The road passed through Ishtar's Gate, the most elaborate entry to the town's fortifications. Its walls were decorated with ceramic reliefs depicting animals. Glazed blue bricks placed next to yellow, white and numerous shades of red bricks created a unique sense of colour, rather different from our modern conception of an urban environment. These colours were complemented by the vivid bright green of many trees and bushes. It is calculated that three to four billion bricks were required for the construction of the outer defensive wall in the middle of

pilgrims walked along Marduk's Avenue to Ishtar's Gate. Babylon was one of the most grandiose towns of its time, in fact, the first real metropolis on Earth. It flourished for nearly 1,500 years, until its decline in the 4th century B.C.

the first millennium B.C., while around eighty-five million bricks were needed for the Tower. These represent just a tiny fraction of the immense task carried out in the relatively short flourishing of the Neo-Babylonian Empire. However, this work could not have been achieved without the labour of thousands of slaves and military captives. Traders and travellers who visited the city also contributed to its fortunes. They brought valuable goods, collected rare art objects and the earliest Mesopotamian relics. The forced and voluntary arrival of multitudes of foreigners into the ancient metropolis might have led to the first 'confounding' of languages attributed to the building of the Tower of Babel.

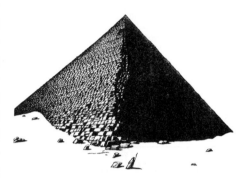

Egyptian Cities

Our knowledge of the history of towns in Egypt is rather different. We know very little about the houses and towns in which the Egyptians lived. Their lives were, in fact, spent 'travelling to the Kingdom of

Death'. They, therefore, devoted more attention to building massive and lasting graves than to building earthly

homes. Ordinary houses were built from clay bricks, reeds, grass and only exceptionally from stone. They disintegrated and disappeared under the drifting sand. However, the graves with piles of food, clothes, jewellery and other objects have been preserved, as well as their model houses for the after-life, which are one piece of knowledge we have about the appearance of an ordinary Egyptian dwelling. 'The Towns of the Dead' near Giza, Sakkara, Zawiyet el-Aryan, Abu Qir, Dahshur, Maydum, Lisht, al-Lahun: the towns of tombs, mastabas and pyramids have survived the centuries. But a perspective on the towns of the living is still missing.

Rather limited archaeological finds and hieroglyphic written records do confirm that towns were already being established in the territory of Egypt from the 4th millennium B.C. These towns were mostly the settlements of free artisans and traders. They

were later conquered by kings who often rebuilt and extended the original built-up areas of towns. The first capital of ancient Egypt was Mennofer, Memphis in Greek, established by King Meni around the year 3000 B.C. From that time, the royal seat was often moved as each ruler was driven by the ambition to establish a new capital. However, a real centre remained

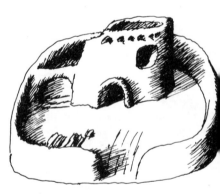

The clay or wooden models of houses found in tombs were inhabited by clay figures. It was as if life continued in them. One can only guess to what extent these models resemble the genuine Egyptian dwellings of that time, for they might represent the dream homes of those departing for the other world.

there, on the borders of Upper and Lower Egypt.

Nowadays, a palm oasis with two villages on its edges stands where the former ancient metropolis of Memphis was situated. Tourist guides draw attention to several finds from relatively unsuccessful excavations. They did not provide many exhibits for the world's museums, and our knowledge of this city, which was among the most famous of the Ancient World, has developed and become more detailed through a slow and difficult process. Now we know that Mennofer did not consist of tightly grouped dwellings, palaces and temples, which is noteworthy in the development of human settlements in history. It was, in a way, an ancient model for our later, so-called 'garden cities'. Palace and temple complexes, military barracks and more or less independent living quarters were spread, like scattered

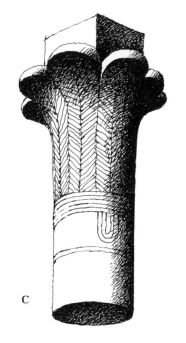

c

Egyptian temple architecture is noted for its columns with capitals whose shape often represented elements of nature, such as the blossoms of papyrus (a) and lotus (b), palm leaves (c), or portrayed the head of Hathor, a fertility goddess (d).

toys, among the parks, fields and orchards. It is said that four hours' brisk walking was needed to reach the other side of the town.

The Egyptian towns grew around the same time as the Mesopotamian towns but the former were significantly different from the latter. These differences have not even been erased over thousands of years. Mennofer, in the period of the Pharaohs, was not a separate world enclosed inside the walls as can be seen in most towns until the end of the 19th century. The rulers of the Nile Valley usually controlled militarily the whole wide area whose natural defensive boundaries were represented by impenetrable

deserts and mountains. Any defensive structures around particular seats of power would have been redundant. The only exceptions were several towns in Upper Egypt. Fields and gardens next to built-up areas removed the dependence on a distant agricultural hinterland. They also made the life of town inhabitants simpler and more pleasant. We can only guess at the motive which drew the Egyptians together and yet enabled them to live on a relatively sparse built-up area. What role was played by practical considerations, such as the need to unite forces when building canals and defensive walls against the Nile's floodwater? Which was of more significance? Tradition, religion, local geographical conditions, technological skills or the economic dependency and the political might of its rulers?

Some of the towns built by

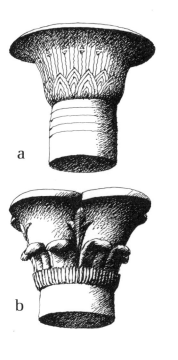

a

b

d

17

The magnificent pyramids of Giza stand at the very edge of the desert; to the right the Pyramid of Cheops, the only one of the Seven Wonders of the World which is preserved till today. This picture provides us with a glimpse of its mysterious, ingeniously contrived interior. Three smaller pyramids of queens are in the foreground. To the left of the road one can see another great structure, the Pyramid of Chephren. A straight ceremonial road from the funereal temple at its foot leads to the dignified Great Sphinx. Scattered around are a number of smaller tombs of relatives, priests, nobles and important personages. Tourists tend to believe that pyramids were huge, isolated monuments, but they were, in fact, components of an ingeniously built-up area, with carefully planned communications and layout. This was a real town—the town of the dead, or necropolis.

the Egyptians are Cinev (This), Mennofer (Memphis), Veset (Thebes), Nennisovet (Heracleopolis), Ictovej (Akanthos), and temple complexes, military barracks and more or less independent living quarters were spread, like scattered Akhetaton, Zoan (Tanis), Pibaste (Bubastis).

In those places where temples, palaces and houses were not used as a 'quarry', that is to say as a source of stone for further construction, or were not swallowed up by the desert, their ruins, such as in

The most important Egyptian towns and burial sites.

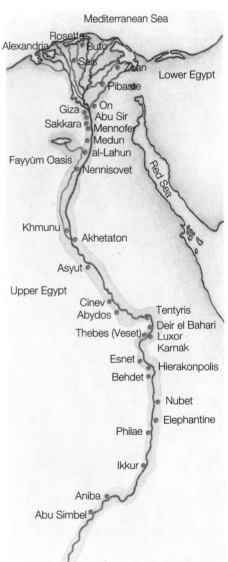

Napoleon Bonaparte's military expedition to Egypt in 1798 resembled, in the view of his contemporaries, a crusade to the Holy Land. The army was accompanied by many scientists, experts in various branches of human knowledge, and this expedition was expected to return with new information about a distant culture which had been veiled in a cloak of secrecy until then. An engraving from that time portrays scientists exploring necropolises which had been engulfed by the desert sand. They could see only the head of the Sphinx protruding from the sand.

Karnak and Luxor near Veset, reveal themselves as monumental architectural structures. With amazing ingenuity and a feeling for the past, ancient builders gradually extended and enlarged older buildings which in each period seemed to be complete and finished. But these only became the foundations of the next development. This building style is termed 'vegetative' construction. A building or even a whole complex grows organically, naturally and only acquires its final apearance over a long period of time.

Three thousand years of changing fortunes left a mark on their appearance as towns flourished or were abandoned. The very shape of towns and settlements founded for the builders of

tombs and pyramids provide evidence of the influence exercised through power struggles and changes in the society. The inhabitants of these towns had different occupations and, more importantly, differing social positions, privileges and obligations. Two examples are Kahun near the Fayyûm Oasis and the settlement by Deir el-Medina. Stonemasons who built the tombs in the Valley of the Kings and the Valley of the Queens lived there.

More reminders of ancient urban settlements have been preserved under the layers of sand near present-day Tell el-Amarna. Amenhotep IV — Akhnaton — built a new capital there in the first half of the 14th century B.C. It was built in the middle of nowhere and

20

after Akhnaton's death its inhabitants deserted their homes. They were never rebuilt or demolished or dismantled for building material to construct new houses. Through their ruins, which point to an ever more elaborate conception, we can observe the very special contribution of Egyptian urbanism in the development of human habitats: next to sophisticated houses surrounded by greenery stood austere and regimented quarters which served as slave labour camps. Without the slaves there would not have been pyramids and the Towns of the Dead; these huge structures survived and overshadowed what seemed to the Pharaohs to be the insignificant and unimportant world of ramshackle slave quarters.

Cities of the Harappian Civilization

The path leading to the discovery of the earliest settlement was not straightforward, but took a circuitous route. As with many other discoveries, it occurred by chance. The brothers John and William Brunton, two ingenious British engineers, faced an apparently simple problem: how to find material to build an embankment for the East Indian Railway in the sandy soil of the Indus valley, with no adjacent quarry. Their clever solution enabled them to acquire gravel at virtually no cost for more than a hundred kilometres of track. They decided

to use burnt bricks from the ruined ancient town of Harappa. This was a practical solution but at the same time had an unfortunate outcome. They effectively buried a major part of the one of the earliest towns on Earth in the structure of the railway embankment. What had survived thousands of years was very nearly obliterated by the railway builders.

The towns of a forgotten civilization in the Indus valley.

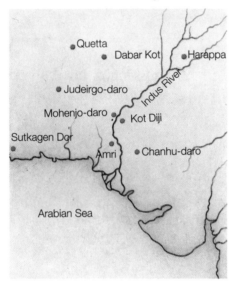

Occasionally the workers found tiny decorated objects among the bricks. Later on, archaeologists were able to study these finds which resembled seals with minute animal and human reliefs alongside indecipherable script. It was established that these finds were artefacts from an unknown civilization which was subsequently named after its place of discovery — the Harappian Civi-

lization. However, for years nobody was interested in this archaeological site. One might say that the builders of the railway stimulated more interest and achieved greater fame than the archaeologists. For many decades steam engines would puff contentedly along the track bearing technical progress on the very embankments built from burnt bricks which were made by people of one of the world's earliest civilizations.

It was only in the 1920s that scientists produced evidence that the people who had created the Harappian culture lived around 2500 B.C. If only Harappa had not been senselessly destroyed! Later, archaeologists discovered a further sixty towns belonging to this civilization. One of them, Mohenjo-daro (the Hill of the Dead),

In the Harappian towns hundreds of seals were discovered scattered among brick fragments. These seals depicted various animals alongside brief inscriptions. The inscriptions have been partially deciphered in recent years. It seems that these seals played an important role in the life of town inhabitants.

Archaeological research of the residential quarter of Mohenjo-daro has confirmed that the town was built according to a plan involving the predetermined direction of streets along the points of the compass. The size of housing blocks and the width of the main and side streets are evident from the excavated foundations and remains of the walls.

was bigger and older than Harappa itself. It was situated about 250 kilometres from the Indus delta. Approximately thirty to a hundred thousand inhabitants might have lived in an area of 2.5 square kilometres.

The discovery of the Harappian civilization surprised the scientific community and also increased our knowledge of the development of human habitats. However, we have only superficial information about the builders of these vast towns. It is mere conjecture or anybody's guess as to where they came from and what language they spoke. The meaning of preserved written records is only being interpreted gradually. However, one day they will undoubtedly provide the answers to many mysteries of life in the Indus valley in the period from 2500 B.C. to 1500 B.C. This is the date when all traces of the Harappian culture disappeared and the towns became deserted.

The archaeological excavations bear witness to an advanced level of urbanization in these first Indian towns. It seems as if they were built according to a pre-determined, and elaborate plan. It is typical of both Harappa and Mohenjo-daro that there was a network of up to ten metre wide streets built along the points of the compass. These streets separated huge living quarters of the same size, 365 × 180 metres, and might have been used to channel traffic into lines. Houses with windowless facades faced the mainstreet while open entrance doors led into a maze of narrow streets, winding through individual housing quarters. These streets must have provided pleasant shade and a retreat from the noise and dust of the main arteries filled with clattering two-wheeled push carts, the most

The uniform network of Mohenjo-daro's main arteries was complemented by narrow, quiet streets leading to individual houses.

Small clay finds—the models of everyday objects—assist in developing theories as to how people lived in the Harappian towns more than three thousand years ago.

common mode of transport at that time.

Contemporary research reveals that the towns of the Harappian civilization had two parts: a living quarter, usually in the shape of a rectangle, and a citadel or a fortress elevated above the city and fortified with walls and towers. The citadel probably housed the municipal administration, the ruler's seat, and the religious centre. In the middle of the Mohenjo-daro citadel there was a spa building. The 12 × 7 metre bathing pool, which was 2.5 metres deep, was probably used during religious rites. Next to it public granaries were built. The ruler of the town might also have been the person who managed these cereal granaries which were the town's greatest assets and were a matter of life and death for the citizens. Archaeologists also discovered an unusually extensive area, which probably acted as an assembly hall. It might also have served as a market, since no other suitable space which could serve this purpose was found within the residential area.

Trade must have prospered in Mohenjo-daro since various artefacts, weighing scales and a variety of seals from the Indus valley reached Mesopotamia.

Chinese Cities

The earliest towns on Earth appeared where power, influence and riches were concentrated. By the second millennium B.C. many more such places existed. In China, one of the earliest was the fortified town of Ao, situated near Zhengzhou in the fertile valley of the Yellow River. From the 14th century B.C. the capital of the Yin Dynasty was situated slightly to the southeast, near the modern town of Anyang. In the 11th century B.C. the Chou Dynasty gained power and united China for the first time. This Dynasty founded a new capital Chao as its power centre. This capital was situated close to the modern town of Sian (Xi'an). In connection with the earliest Chinese towns we might also refer to one of the earliest, or maybe even the first, manual on town planning — an architectural treatise, Kchao-kung-t'i. It was part of the Chou Dynasty's ritual book. Among other pieces of advice it recommended that a town should have a square design, be dissected by nine main streets leading from north to south and nine main streets leading from east to west. The streets' width should be nine widths of a chariot. The walls surrounding a square town were to be interrupted by three gates on each side. According to this treatise, the town should be dominated by the ruler's palace with a courtyard, temples and a market square. It was also recommended that a town should be established in such a way that it was protected by mountains to the north, and had a river flowing on its southern boundary.

Mediterranean Cities

By the year 2000 B.C. the original Neolithic settlements around the Aegean Sea and on Crete had developed into towns. Knossos, the ancient city of Crete, occupied an exceptional place between the years 1800–1550 B.C. Its fall around the beginning of the 14th century B.C. resulted from a natural disaster, internal disputes or a hostile attack by the Achaeans. An idea of what the ancient Cretan towns looked like is difficult to form from the ruins. The best preserved small town is Gournia in the eastern part of the island. It was situated on a hill, interwoven with irregular streets, already paved with cobblestones in the 16th century B.C. The different levels of the individual streets were connected by staircases. The inhabitants built their houses from clay bricks, and they seem to have had central water supplies as ceramic drainage pipes were also excavated. Our notion of the Cretan towns is confirmed only by a few earthenware plaques from King Minos's palace at Knossos. When Arthur John Evans, an English archaeologist, discovered these plaques he was particularly interested in the depiction of a fortified town with decorated house facades. However, the windows with four to six panels made of transparent material were the biggest surprise. In contrast to earlier Sumerian towns, these town houses were the first facing the daily light.

Lava and volcanic dust have best conserved and preserved the earliest habitats. After a volcanic eruption time stood still in houses and streets and everything remained intact. Something like that happened on the Aegean island of Thera in the 16th century B.C. Excavations carried out in the 1970s confirmed that its civilization was similar to the Minoan civilization in Crete. This helped to complete our theories of how people lived in the towns of the Mediterranean, the cradle of European culture. Archaeologists discovered town houses with their decorations, furniture, coloured murals depicting landscape; women and girls in festive clothing; fishermen with their catch; military expeditions; exotic plants and animals. They also portray customs, the environment in which people lived, and many interesting details of daily life. A successful maritime trade (even piracy) brought them wealth. Municipal houses matched the seats of rulers in splendour. Excavations showed that maritime trade promoted an extraordinary flourishing of the Bronze Age town.

The Phoenicians, a Semitic people who inhabited Phoenicia, an ancient country along the coast of the eastern Mediterranean (modern Lebanon), also owed their wealth to the sea. The towns of Tyre, Sidon and especially Byblos became famous. Byblos gained its reputation not only for its prosperity and imposing buildings but specifically for a most important invention related to this town — the invention of the alphabet, which became fundamental to the development of human civilization.

The Phoenicians could not support themselves other than by navigation and trade. Byblos was an important metropolis from the 3rd millennium B.C. Vessels laden with goods from Egypt, Mesopotamia and Anatolia entered its port. The Phoenicians needed to off-load or even store cargoes during their voyages and thus they established new coastal towns. During their construction they used all the knowledge they had acquired during their travels. They handled cargoes and products of the most advanced nations of the ancient world, and thus had the opportunity to get to know and to adopt the ways of other civilizations and cultures.

Around 1200 B.C. when they were looking for a more accurate and faster means of keeping accounts of their trade, they drew on knowledge gathered by the Egyptians and compiled the first letter alphabet composed of consonants. This alphabet made possible the development of a literature.

Phoenician Byblos provides evidence that towns which serve as crossing points, where goods, opinions and knowledge are all exchanged, also promote new ideas and lead to new inventions. The brisk trade which drew various nationalities from far and near to Byblos also contributed to the spread of the new letter alphabet. It was soon adopted by the Jews, it spread into the ancient Greek towns, and it was through the Etruscans that the Greek alphabet, with added vowels, reached the Romans. These means of disseminating the alphabet are in many aspects similar to the ways by which the art of town planning dispersed and developed. We will see that when we pass through the following Gateway to municipal areas.

The towns of Crete grew rich from maritime trade; their defence and wealth were guaranteed by a strong navy. Their houses were made of brick and cut stone, and many of them were multi-storey. Cretan towns boasted magnificent palaces, complete with central water supplies and drainage. The picture portrays what the façade leading to the courtyard of the famous palace at Knossos might have looked like.

25

In Addition

Were Kathleen Kenyon and James Mellaart right when they claimed to have uncovered the foundations of the first cities and not the remains of agricultural settlements under the layers of soil and stone?

There is no easy answer to this question. In clarifying the origins of urban civilization, using ancient ruins and archaeological finds as guides, we are also getting nearer to a definition of what, in fact, makes the city different from other settlements. What changes did the city undergo? What is a city?

The lengthy discussions of archaeologists and historians about the giving the status of city to a human habitat hidden under the layers of soil, thousands of years old, have identified fundamental conditions with which a settlement should comply. It should be added that Jericho and Çatal Hüyük have displayed these signs in principle at the very beginning of urban development.

The first pre-condition calls for evidence that it was a permenent settlement and that people lived there for a period of time. Second-

What, in fact, is a town, . . . and how does it develop?

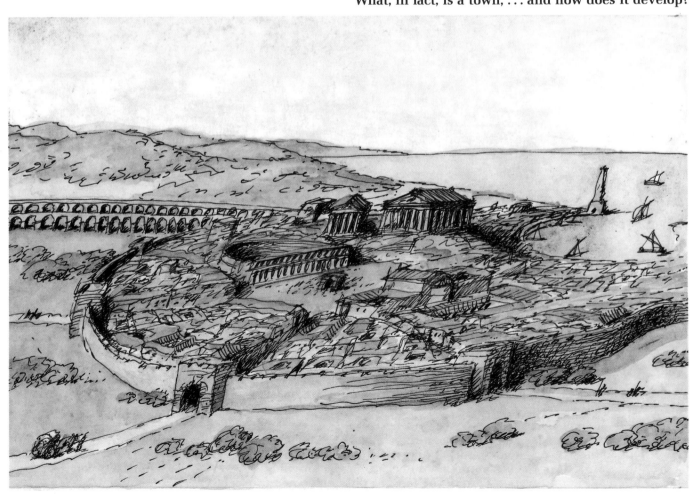

ly, a large number of people had to be united inside a defined living area. The inhabitants of cities usually specialized in a certain activity, trade or craft. The buildings, whether homes or for social or religious purposes, had a characteristic architectural style which was typical for the given locality. In the town there were urban establishments and buildings, such as granaries, fortifications and roads. In later towns there were also sewage systems and water supplies which indicated a more sophisticated organization of public life. Cities also had to be important for people living outside them, in a wider area, in contrast with agricultural settlements which served only the local needs of their inhabitants. However, this relationship was reciprocal — the city was as dependent on its immediate and more distant environment. Therefore, the cities were often founded at the crossroads of trade routes or close to ports which linked them with more distant settlements.

A Guide to the Historical Labyrinth

35000—8th millennium B.C. — The period when modern man (Homo sapiens fossilis) appeared; production technology developed; the division of labour was introduced followed by the exchange of goods.

9000 B.C. — At about this time the first settlements with permanent dwellings appeared in the hilly areas of the Middle East.

8th millennium B.C. — The existence of Jericho in Palestine considered to be the earliest settlement of the urban type; Kathleen Kenyon, a British archaeologist, discovered this so-called Pre-ceramic City in the 1950s. According to some, Jericho already existed before the 9th millennium B.C.

6500—5700 B.C. — The beginnings of Çatal Hüyük in Anatolia date from this period. It was discovered in the early 1960s by James Mellaart.

6th—5th millennium B.C — Agriculture developed in the fertile valleys of the rivers Euphrates and Tigris, later in the valleys of the Nile and the Indus; the creation of pre-conditions for the development of urban civilizations.

3500—3000 B.C. — The Sumerians settled in Mesopotamia; the earliest Sumerian written records appeared.

— The origins of the Sumerian city states — Ur, Uruk, Eridu.

c. 3000 B.C. — King Meni established Mennofer (Memphis), the first capital of a united Egypt.

2800—2400 B.C. — The flourishing of Sumerian cities.

2700—2270 B.C. — The period of the Old Kingdom in Egypt; the greatest pyramids were built, which with tombs create Towns of Dead.

2500—1500 B.C. — Mohenjo-daro, Harappa — the towns of the Harappian civilization in the Indus valley.

2000—1550 B.C. — The urban type settlements appeared around splendid palaces in Crete; the Middle Minoan Period.

1800—1100 B.C. — The urban seats of the Yin Dynasty in China.

1792—1750 B.C. — Babylon became the most important city of Mesopotamia under the reign of Hammurabi, the fifth ruler of the Old Babylonian Empire.

1500 B.C. — The earliest town plan depicting Nippur, an early Sumerian cultural centre, dates from this time.

1600—1200 B.C. — The flourishing of Mycenae, Pylos, Tiryns during the zenith of the Mycenaean civilization.

c. 1200 B.C. — A letter alphabet invented in the Phoenician town of Byblos.

II *A Gateway into Ancient Times*

We now approach a Gateway through which we can enter urban space. Much seems to have changed in the course of the centuries: the façades of the buildings, clothing, the range of transport, people's behaviour and thinking.

However, despite all the radical attempts to alter the appearance of towns, many features remain unchanged. It is true that in line with new requirements, the views differ concerning the size of squares, the directions and width of streets, the area and density of settlement.

European towns embraced the knowledge developed over generations, and adapted it to new conditions. Their histories are tales told umpteen times, with individual plots and language but a common fundamental basis.

Similarly to many literary plots whose origins can be traced back to ancient myth and legend, we might also gain a better understanding of the changes in urban areas if we return through this Gateway into the cities and towns of antiquity.

Ancient Greek Cities

The most famous period in the existence of Greek city states was preceeded by a development which was not unified but took place in stages. Nevertheless, it provides an insight into the origins from which European culture grew. In the 2nd millennium B.C. the Greek tribes, especially the Achaeans, the Aeolians, the

The Entrance Gate of the Palace of Mycenae, Peloponnesus, with the typical triangular aperture above the entrance in which was mounted what is probably the earliest known monumental sculpture on European territory.

Ionians and the Dorians, settled around the Aegean Sea. Their names live on in various architectural orders.

In the first period, in Homeric Greece (up to the 8th century B.C.), the Greeks conquered the native inhabitants and utilized their knowledge, such as the building skills of the Mycenaean civilization. An irregular coastal landscape and ethnic differences led to the establishment of smaller city states whose power was concentrated in towns. Independent rival city states, such as Sparta, Athens, Corinth and Thebes, were founded.

A map of the ancient Greek cities and important town settlements in the Aegean region.

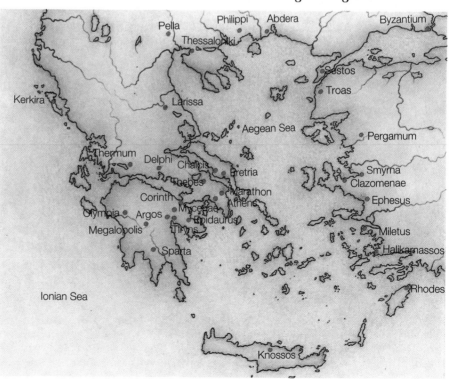

The Greeks walked along the main street which crossed the agora diagonally; they passed Zeus's Stoa, and the Odeon, or covered theatre, in the centre of the agora. To the left, they passed the Attala Stoa, and then climbed to the Acropolis above the city, which was dominated by the Parthenon, a Doric temple. This is how Athens must have looked in the 2nd century B.C.

34

Later, in the so-called Archaic Period (7th—6th centuries B.C.), many stone buildings, especially temples, were built in towns. Greece was a maritime superpower, particularly the Ionians. They settled in Attica, an ancient Greek district of which Athens was the capital, and founded town colonies on the shores of the Black and Aegean Seas.

The history of Ancient Greece lies in the history of the foundation, the rise and the extinction of its towns.

Although the Classical period of Greek history (5th—4th centuries B.C.) started with the Persian attack on Athens and the destruction of the Acropolis in 480 B.C., a new magnificent construction of Athens followed soon after the Persians' defeat. It was also the era when the struggle for the supremacy of city states over Greece reached its zenith.

And we can pursue this line of enquiry. The Hellenistic period (4th—1st centuries B.C.) began with the death of Alexander the Great, King of Macedon, who led the Greek armies in the war against Persia, and greatly extended the power of Greece. It was a period in which their arts, philosophy and science flourished. This period embraces an exceptional expansion and also the decline of towns.

The knowledge of historians combined with contemporary literature inform us that the ancient Greeks enriched the architecture of towns by giving them a new dimension: they developed social and

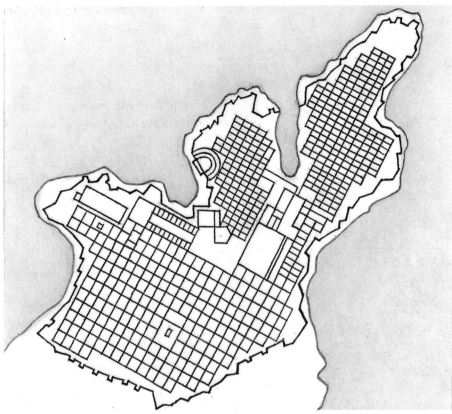

A Greek house with the central courtyard, in which family life was concentrated. It was usually built from brick, later from stone, and was occasionally multi-storey; usually facing the street with a windowless façade.

The plan of Miletus with its typical street network which embraces the system of public areas and important buildings—agoras, a theatre, a stadium and a port. The checkerboard composition made possible the rapid and economic reconstruction of older towns or the construction of new towns. This was undoubtedly the reason why this design provided ample inspiration to urban planners and architects many centuries later, for example when establishing new towns on the American continent in the 18th and 19th centuries.

There are obvious parallels between the ground-plan of Miletus and the original plan of Washington, D.C., designed by Pierre Ch. L'Enfant in 1791.

communal life. This was facilitated by a strong democratic element in society; the greater participation of free citizens in the management and decision-making in public affairs. The need to meet regularly in assemblies significantly affected the layout and organization of towns. In addition to a religious centre, such as the Acropolis in Athens, the agora, a spacious and usually rectangular central square, acquired a new role. Homer in his epic poem the *Iliad* describes the agora as an assembly point, a place where people exchanged views and opinions, discussed important issues, resolved common problems, and conducted their trade.

In the Classical Period, the agora played a key rôle. It was bordered on at least one side by a stoa, a form of colonnade or a covered portico, which provided shelter from the elements; the sun, the rain and the wind. Citizens walked there, seeking amusement, or conversation; poets recited their poems; philosophers conducted their learned discussions. The agora also contained a theatre, a public spa and a library, and exhibitions were held there. Citizens going to hold important discussions at, for example, the town hall or court, walked across the agora. It was also a place which attracted numerous traders with their stalls, while artisan workshops and taverns were situated nearby.

The lively atmosphere drew crowds to this place at all times of the day. The ambience of the town centre was enhanced by magnificent architecture, statues and columns, behind which individual figures moved gracefully. There were also objects to amuse and edify the citizens, sun dials, weathercocks and fountains. The agora in the seaside town of Priene was rectangular (75 × 46 metres), surrounded on all its sides by colonnades. It gave the impression of a large roofless living room.

The city did not, however,

The propensity of the Greeks to build towns is also shown in their plan for Mount Athos on the Khalkidhiki peninsula. This mountain figured several times in the Persian wars. In addition, it almost became famous for another reason: Deinocrates, Alexander the Great's adviser for town building (he assisted in drawing up many town plans, including that of Alexandria), suggested that a statue of a giant whose hand would support a town for ten thousand inhabitants be carved into the mighty cliff of Mount Athos. This plan was never carried out as there was not sufficient agricultural hinterland for the settlement. If built, Mount Athos would have become a rare monument celebrating cities which for centuries remained the repository of Greek culture.
J. B. Fischer von Erlach, an important Austrian architect, returned to this tale of an unbuilt city in the early 18th century. For his *Entwurf einer historischen Architektur* (History of World Architecture) he made an engraving of an idealized reconstruction of a 4th century B.C. town situated on Mount Athos.

consist only of its main square. What were the surroundings like? Was the town established in a random, unplanned manner and grew organically? Or was it founded according to a unified plan, with a clear urban role in mind? In the case of the Greek cities we can observe a certain rivalry between these two approaches to town building and the design of town spaces. And these two approaches still maintain their significance in urban planning today.

Each of these approaches

has its advantages and disadvantages; its advocates and opponents. The former offers a greater variety and diversity; it is based on tradition; it adapts street directions and the shape of the square to local conditions, to the natural features of the terrain; it is also technically and financially less demanding. On the other hand, those settlements which were founded from scratch, according to a set plan and with no expense spared, could guarantee a functioning transport system, which was a very

The shape of column capitals on Greek and Roman buildings and temples enables us to determine the architectural style in which they were built. Throughout the ages architecture has been inspired by or incorporated Greek and Roman architectural styles. The first in line is the Doric capital, which is relatively simple and unpretentious but distinguished by its massive strength. The most famous Doric temple is the Parthenon on the Athenian Acropolis. The second is the Ionic capital, which is more subtle and is distinguished by its volute. The third is the Corinthian capital, which is highly ornate and was mainly used by the Romans.

important consideration for the more populous cities. A well thought out design and a clear geometrical composition makes an impressive impact, even though it can diminish the subjective appeal of diverse surroundings.

The Ancient Greek cities usually combined these two approaches. At first they were characterized by an irregular network of streets. Whole generations of builders concentrated their attention on the town centre, the main street and the agora. They built temples, public buildings and shops. The rest of the town grew organically according to the needs of its inhabitants. This is especially true of Athens.

On the other hand, newly founded towns, town colonies, established to improve trade and protect military con-

quests, were built according to a precise urban plan. One example is the regular checkerboard ground-plan of Miletus, an ancient Greek city in Asia Minor. The city's reconstruction was supervised by Hippodamus of Miletus. Since then this checkerboard town layout, named the Hippodamian plan, has spread. It made new towns easy to build and survey. The advantages of this arrangement were especially appreciated by 18th and 19th century town planners and were adopted, for example, when building new towns in the USA.

The strict grid plan of streets imposed discipline and order upon ancient Greek cities such as Rhodes, Priene, Pergamum, Ephesus and Alexandria. Despite the observance of such strict geometric patterns, these newly founded

towns gave the impression of diversity and variety. Undoubtedly, one of the reasons was the fact that such clear geometric composition required that simple, architecturally impressive buildings filled the urban space.

Rome

The fame of Ancient Greece supposedly declined with its conquest by Rome, its stronger and more aggressive rival. However, the knowledge of Greek town builders provided inspiration in later centuries. The climax of Roman building and architecture, which draws on the Greek tradition, occurred towards the end of the Roman Republic. At the time Rome was indeed becoming a really vast city. Towards the end of the 2nd century and at the beginning of the 1st cen-

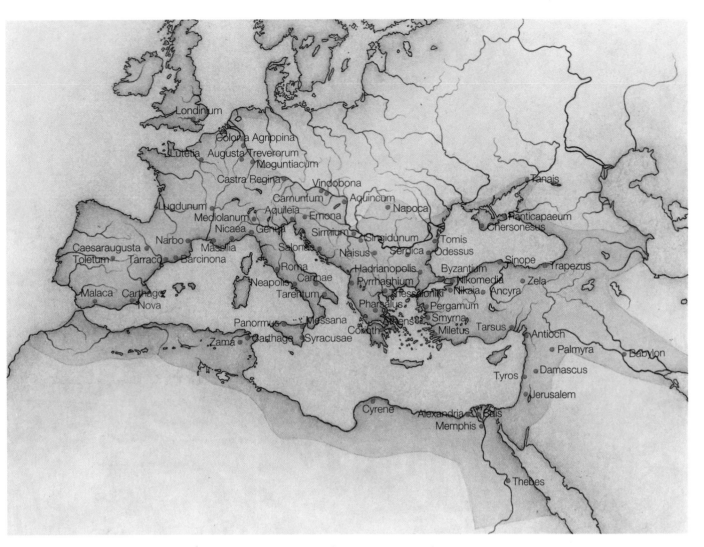

A map of towns and important military camps in the Roman Empire.

Victory arches, or triumphal arches were built by the Romans to commemorate important events, especially military conquests. They can be found not only in Rome but also in many other cities of the Roman Empire. They differ in size; they are divided by columns and decorated with reliefs and sculptures.

A view of the centre of Rome between the 1st and 3rd centuries as seen from Tabularium, or the state archives, over to the Arch of Septimus Severus, the Forum Romanum and upwards to the Colosseum.

tury B.C. Rome gradually conquered ever larger and more distant territories; it was a period of high-profile military campaigns and battles, but also a period in which literature, the arts and architecture flourished. The conquered territories and colonies provided ample financial revenue, building materials and labour; they also enriched art collections with their objects. Military successes dazzled the victors and gave them a feeling of superiority and power; they also fired their ambition to live in the most beautiful city on Earth.

The Romans succeeded in fulfilling this ambition due to the fact that building skills were at their peak. The builders of Rome employed the knowledge and architectural skills which had developed over the centuries. They mastered complex constructions and the more advanced technology of building. They learnt to express their ideas on town planning in complex and sophisticated relationships. They often copied the Greeks in this respect. Their inspiration was at times rather blatant. Numerous statues which decorated municipal and private houses often came directly from Ancient Greek cities. The Romans not only admired the Greeks, but defeated them and carried off their works of art as military prizes.

The most splendid reconstruction in the centre of Rome was carried out during the reign of Gaius Julius Caesar (100—44 B.C.). The emperor realized that the hectic life of the metropolis could no longer be contained within the area of the old town centre. He bought up huge plots of land next to the Forum Romanum, the oldest centre of social life in Rome, and had a new Forum, the Forum Iulium or Forum Caesarum, built there. He also initiated the construction of other buildings, such as the spacious citizens' assembly on the Martian Field. However, many of his more ambitious plans were only realized by his successor, Gaius Octavius Augustus.

The re-birth of Rome from 'a town made of brick' (or rather 'made of wood') into a tiled and marble-decorated city continued. A new forum, the Forum Augustum, was built. The Emperor Augustus also insisted that other military leaders and rich citizens should expend seized treasures on the erection of municipal buildings. For example, his son-in-law, Marcus Agrippa, had a new Roman aqueduct built at his own expense. The overcrowded Imperial Rome consumed 1,000,000 cubic metres of water daily.

Rome was an attractive city in which to live. In addition to various advantages, rights and freedoms, its citizens were also entitled to cheaper flour, bread rations and free access to games and shows held in the Amphitheatre and circuses.

Rome and individual stages of its construction throughout the centuries.

probably inhabited area

structures of the Republican Period

structures of Augustan reconstruction

structures dating from A.D. 14 to 250

ancient buildings of the latter period

= aqueducts

A shop sign of a Rome trader selling vegetables and poultry; a 2nd century relief.

Greek and Roman furniture.

In addition to splendid town houses, luxurious suburban villas and magnificent palaces for Roman Emperors were built. This is the reconstructed villa of the Emperor Hadrian at Tivoli, near Rome.

(*cohortes urbanae*) supervised and enforced law and order, which was a very important service as ancient Rome suffered from crime as much as other metropolises. At the beginning of this millennium life was busier than ever before in its squares, in its wide streets, in its theatres and arenas. A remarkable urban complex of connecting Imperial squares appeared at the time. These squares were planned and defined areas surrounded by stoas, statues and important buildings. In addition to the Forum Caesarum and the Forum Augustum, the Forum of Vespasian (ruled A.D. 69—79), the Forum of the Emperor Nerva (A.D. 96—98) and the largest of all, the Forum of Trajan (A.D. 98—117), were added. Important achievements and military conquests were commemorated in public places and the crossroads of main streets by erecting triumphal arches and columns. Entire generations of builders turned central Rome into a unique urban composition, which typified the contemporary concepts of town architecture.

There is relatively little remaining now of these buildings and structures, both great and small. Much has been destroyed by war, fire, earthquakes, and also by unscrupulous builders who used dilapidated buildings as a convenient and profitable source of materials for new buildings. The remaining ancient Roman buildings provide an enchanting romantic background for the modern city.

The city's growth required a sophisticated administration system. For example, the first ever municipal fire service was established there. At the turn of the millennium Rome had seven fire brigades (*cohortes vigilum*) consisting of 1,000 members.

The so-called 'city divisions'

Despite that, we know more about ancient Rome and other Roman cities than about many later towns. The Romans themselves contributed to our knowledge through their military expansionism combined with their remarkable cultural impact on their neighbours. Those buildings and structures which did not survive in Rome have been preserved in other Italian towns or even in distant provinces. A uniquely detailed testimony to life nearly two thousand years ago was provided by the excavations in the towns of Pompeii, Stabiae and Herculaneum in Campania, Italy. These towns were buried by lava and volcanic dust in A.D. 79. Everyday objects were recovered intact and murals and inscriptions on walls were discovered in the Pompeian houses. These provide an insight into everyday life in a typical town. The two main streets, which were enclosed by colonnades, met in the main square. There was a smallish forum with an assembly hall for the town council, basilicas and temples. A dense network of small streets, generally paved, with shops and artisan workshops, joined with the main streets.

Literature allows us to understand better the town's architecture and spaces. Roman libraries contained philosophical treatises, economic records, poetry, dramas and historical works. This is a substantial literary legacy, which reflects the Romans' relationship with the surrounding world, and obviously with the

In his writings on architecture, at the very beginning of the chapter on town building, Vitruvius stresses that it is vital to select the healthiest site available. With reference to his text, Renaissance architects designed the ideal diagram of a perfect city, which they added to Vitruvius's *Ten Books on Architecture*.

An attempt to reconstruct one of Vitruvius's buildings mentioned in his *Ten Books on Architecture*: a cross section of Vitruvius's Basilica at Fano shows the perfectly symmetrical design of the building.

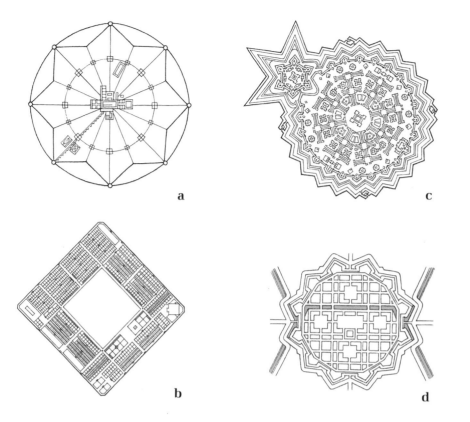

a

c

b

d

Several ground-plans for ideal cities:
Filarète's design from the first half of the 15th century is probably the first depiction of a star-shaped Renaissance town (a).
Albrecht Dürer's regular layout of 1527 is reminiscent, in many aspects, of Gothic town ground-plans (b).
Jaques François Perret — this complex ornamental drawing from 1601 is the precursor of later Baroque designs; a tower house stands in the centre of the city (c).
In his design of 1615 Vincenzo Scamozzi combines the rectangular and star layouts of the city with a canal flowing through it (d).

cities as well. Marcus Vitruvius Pollio, a Roman architect, wrote the first comprehensive encyclopaedia of architecture *De architectura* in 25 B.C.

No other work has so significantly influenced further development in its field as those ten books by Vitruvius. Imperial Rome fell into decay after the fall of the Roman Empire in the 5th century A.D.; formerly famous cities became depopulated, desolated and ruined; the centres of power shifted away. *De architectura* preserved the concepts of the houses, palaces and temples, thus securing the continuity of European architecture. In the Middle Ages, builders gained technological expertise and instruction from this encyclopaedia. When the Renaissance revived an interest in the Classical times, Vitruvius's treatise led to further study of architectural styles and urban layout.

The Renaissance poets Dante and Petrarch rediscovered the treasures of Classical Roman poetry for their contemporaries after a thousand year gap. Inspired by the magnificent and rational urbanism of ancient cities, the Renaissance architects planned their ideal towns. However, these were just grandiose schemes and

Many precisely executed urban designs appeared in the Renaissance period. However, only a few of them were realized in strict accordance with their plans which aimed at an ideal urban composition. Palma Nuova, founded in the late 16th century, is one of the best known cities built at this time.

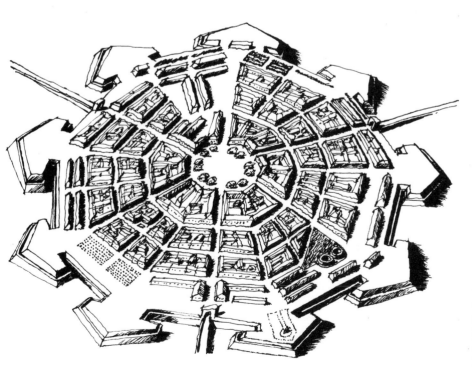

Ground-plans of several famous European town squares. The shapes of the squares and the way streets are aligned to them are often strange. However, some were built strictly according to plan, whereas elsewhere the builders followed the direc-

Modena —
Piazza Grande

Catania —
Piazza San Filippo

Reims —
Place Royale

Ostia —
Forum Caesarum

Edinburgh —
Charlotte Square

Lucca —
Piazza del Marcato

Stuttgart —
Königstraße

Vienna —
Neuer Markt

Siena —
San Virgilio

Catania —
Piazza Dante

tions of earlier roads, the contours of the terrain and the arrangement of previously built-up spaces around traditional market places or historically important sites.

Stuttgart —
Österreichischer Platz

London —
Regent's Park

Paris —
Place des Victoires

Ludwigsburg —
Marktplatz

Paris —
Place Dauphine

Versailles —
Place Dauphine

London —
Hanover Square

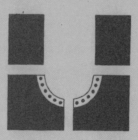

London —
Park Crescent

Rome —
Piazza Navona

Kassel —
Königsplatz

dreams for a utopian urban environment, which was composed of an elaborated mosaic of houses, palaces, streets and squares, with the walls strictly defining and separating the urban space from the wider countryside.

With hindsight we can appreciate how human conceptions vary, whether they concern a perfect scale for towns, their size or the most convenient layout. We have a different perception of the atmosphere of streets and squares and our pace of life is also different. Large spaces, which might look grandiose, dignified and magnificent in the architect's plan, might evoke in us feelings of confinement and restriction. The face of a town and the changes it undergoes also depend on the expense lavished on reconstruction and new construction.

A 17th century plan of Amsterdam provides evidence that Renaissance ideas had an impact on the construction of this city which has remained one of the most important European centres since the 16th century.

In Addition

The knowledge and experience of Roman town builders provide us now with an insight into the variety and diversity of this man-made environment. For example, there was a connected complex of squares: a network of the main streets linking the squares and narrow streets with marketplaces and smaller squares. These squares varied as to size, shape and position; their 'furnishings' differed as well according to the purpose for which they were used by their inhabitants.

A look at the centre of ancient Rome provokes the very same questions which are asked when talking about modern cities: What should a city look like and what are its typical features? How do individual towns differ from one another at first glance? What are the basic rules by which the urban spaces divide, interlink or separate? Why does one town seem to be tightly grouped while another one appears to be dispersed over a wide area?

Urban spaces differ not only in size and position but also in the rôle which they play in their inhabitants' lives. It was already possible in ancient Rome to differentiate public spaces, such as squares of various sizes and shapes, which could be used for ceremonial purposes, in contrast to spaces used as marketplaces. Roman public spaces were built in such a way as to convey an impression of grandeur.

Streets are an integral part of any town. They provide transport links connecting the individual parts of the town and contribute to a sense of direction. The streets are of varying width, which might reflect their social importance, but more often reflects how much traffic they carry. The public areas of streets and squares are delineated by houses, palaces and other buildings, which are often grouped into town blocks.

In Rome in addition to freely accessible public spaces, we pass by the spaces reserved for selected groups of people, such as palace courtyards, backyards and gardens. However, we can see that public and private areas often overlapped and intermingled. Stoas, or colonnades, on the Greek agora or the Roman forum, are a typical example. Man is simultaneously outdoors and indoors, in the intimate security of a building, protected against the elements but at the same time close to public life. In the 19th century the builders of spa towns rediscovered the advantages of a similar space arrangement.

However, the role assigned to each particular space in the town does not only depend on the purpose it fulfils (e.g. public assembly, trade, production, leisure and amusement). It also depends on the inhabitants' attitude to it, which reflects the atmosphere of particular places. Some places attract people through some form of indefinable charm whereas others might repel visitors owing to their austere and gloomy atmosphere.

Urban areas. They are viewed and utilized in many different ways. Their shape, size, and how they used to be equipped correspond to the importance of each respective area in the structure of town composition.

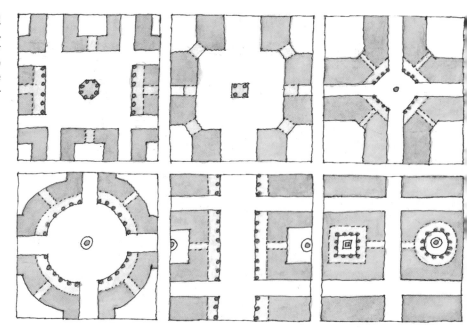

A Guide to the Historical Labyrinth

From the 8th century B.C. — The strengthening of the power of Greek city states; the great Greek colonization;
— the foundation of towns in southern Italy, on the northern coast of Africa and on the Black Sea coast.

753 B.C. — According to legend the founding of Rome by Romulus and Remus. However the settlements on the hills probably became a town under the Etruscan influence in the 7th—6th centuries B.C.

605—562 B.C. — Babylon, destroyed countless times by hostile armies, reached the height of its power, during the Neo-Babylonian Empire under Nebuchadnezzar II.

6th century B.C. — The Etruscans, who had settled in central Italy before the 8th century B.C., created a federation of twelve city states [Veii, Caere, Tarquinia, Pisae...] and held political power over a vast territory.

c. 510 B.C. — According to legend, the Etruscan kings were expelled from Rome and the Republic was founded.

480—430 B.C. — The zenith of Athenian democracy, art and the Greek building craft, the 'Golden Age' of Athens.

450 B.C. — Miletus, an ancient Greek city in Asia Minor, was re-built on a grid plan.

380 B.C. — Plato, the Greek philosopher, wrote his 'Laws'. This doctrine provided inspiration for later philosophers to consider the ideal system of society's organization.

332—331 B.C. — Alexander the Great established Alexandria, a grandiose metropolis built according to a plan. At the beginning of the Christian era it became the cultural and learning centre of the Ancient World.

312 B.C. — The Via Appia connected Rome with southern Italy, the first of the important roads which later enabled Rome to spread its military and economic power.

the end of the 2nd century B.C. — Early technology in what is modern Bohemia in central Europe was concentrated in large fortified settlements resembling towns, e.g. Celtic oppidums: the largest Celtic oppidum occupied an exceptionally large area of 170 hectares on the right bank of the River Vltava.

from the middle of the 1st to 2nd century A.D. — The peak of construction in Rome and Roman towns; imperial forums and other public buildings were erected.

c. 25 B.C. — Marcus Vitruvius Pollio wrote his ten-volume theoretical work De architectura which included fundamental ideas on town construction.

A.D. 79 — Lava and volcanic dust from nearby Mount Vesuvius buried three flourishing towns — Pompeii, Herculaneum and Stabiae.

2nd century — An urban settlement on the river island of La Venta in eastern Mexico was abandoned; its origins date back to the 14th century B.C.; it belonged to the pre-Mayan civilization.

A.D. 335 — Constantinople, erected where the Greek colony of Byzantium stood, became the new capital of the Roman Empire; the Slavs named it 'Cařihrad'; it was conquered by the

Turks in the 15th century and later re-named Istanbul.

A.D. 365 — An earthquake (one of many in this region) destroyed several flourishing eastern Mediterranean towns.

A.D. 452 — The Huns invaded and pillaged towns on the Adriatic coast of Italy; the original inhabitants found a safe haven in the lagoons and founded Venice, which became a prosperous and grand city in the first half of the 2nd millennium owing to her commercial and cultural links with Europe and countries further to the East.

III *A Gateway to City Planners and Builders*

Workers repairing a sewage system in one of the streets of Mexico City made a remarkable discovery two metres under a pavement. As so often in history, this occurred purely by chance, on a February day in 1978. A round stone, four metres in diameter, with the carved head of a woman and a variety of hands, feet, arms and legs, had remained for centuries in a place which archaeologists would rarely, if ever, excavate. It was a ritual stone — the Coyolxauhqui. It depicts the murdered Goddess of the Moon. This stone is said to have been situated among the paving stones of an Aztec temple.

This discovery became the turning point in unveiling the city's history, which had until then been shrouded in mystery. The temple itself was at the centre of the legendary Aztec seat of Tenochtitlán, on whose foundations, or ruins, the modern Mexico City was established (and has developed ever since).

The Aztecs reached the valley of Mexico around A.D. 1250. They adopted and further developed the cultural legacy of advanced American civilizations, especially that of the Toltecs, who in turn, had drawn on their knowledge of civilization from the nearby Teotihuacan.

The Tenochtitlán Aztecs were members of a poor but militant tribe, notorious for thieving. They were looking for a safe haven and decided to settle on a boggy island situated on Lake Texcoco. Its unusual geographical situation forced them to use some ingenious technology for urban construction. In fact, their urban development is unique and provides evidence for a variety of influences on the building skills of our ancestors.

The Aztecs lowered wickerwork baskets filled with soil and plant seedlings into the lake. The plants' roots embedded themselves in the lake bed and grew so that an area of dry land gradually appeared at the surface. Houses, temples and palaces were built there. The poor inhabitants built houses from rush, plastered with wattle; more ambitious dwellings were made of sun-dried bricks while the walls of important buildings were built of volcanic rock. The town was divided into four quarters which were connected with the mainland by causeways. Canals were built parallel to these causeways and ended at the main square from which the main water pipelines distributed water into the individual town districts. The square was domi-

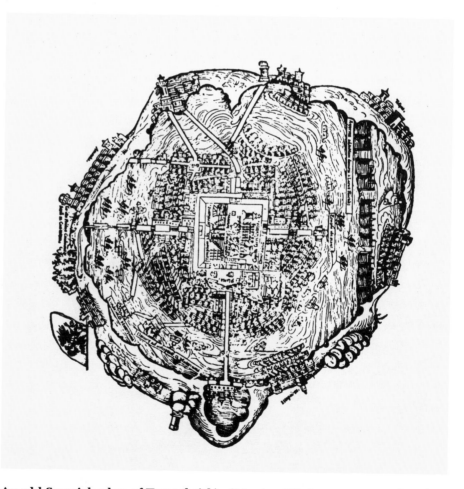

An old Spanish plan of Tenochtitlán (Mexico City) on an engraving dating from 1524 which illustrates the first edition of the Latin translation (in Nuremberg) of Cortés's Second Report on his Transatlantic Expedition, *Praeclara Ferdinandi Cortesii de Nova Maris Oceani Hyspania Narratio.*

nated by a sixty metre high pyramid of temples and palaces which towered over hundreds of Aztec huts huddled together. Canoes transported foodstuffs and goods from the mainland; they passed through the canals and under wooden drawbridges which linked shining white houses. The whole man-made island was surrounded by the rich green of floating gardens.

'Looking at that splendid image, we were lost for words; wondering if what we saw was real . . .'. This was how Bernal Díaz del Castillo saw Tenochtitlán as late as 1519: '. . . a huge Mexican city stood in front of us and . . . we counted a mere four hundred soldiers.'

The blue surface of Lake Texcoco might have reflected around one hundred thousand houses, home to a quarter to half a million inhabitants; many times more than Paris or London of that time. However, those few hundred of Hernán Cortés's soldiers, including Bernal Díaz del Castillo, left not stone unturned in the Aztecs' metropolis.

The city of Teotihuacán turned into fascinating, but deserted, ruins long before the Aztecs reached Central Mexico. The city flourished for more than one thousand years. It was built on a plateau, 7,500 feet above sea level. An attempt to reconstruct it as it might have looked at its zenith indicates its builders' vision. Teotihuacán began to decline in the 6th century A.D.; its inhabitants were leaving the city for reasons unknown to us; in the 8th and 9th centuries the buildings were abandoned and the city was left without any sign of life.

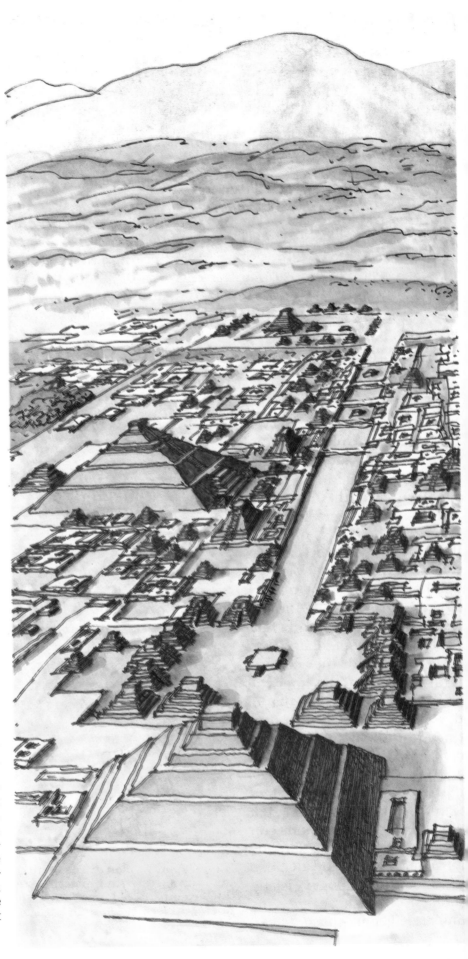

If we had not had evidence about the existence of this remarkable floating town, which has been both painstakingly pieced together and fortuitously discovered by Mexican archaeologists and historians, we might have been inclined to dismiss stories about this Mexican Venice as a legend or sheer invention.

At the end of the Middle Ages, the conquistadores gazed with amazement at Tenochtitlán. No European metropolis could match its population. The city's appearance as well as the way it had been built and its building materials bore no comparison. This was an encounter of two completely different worlds, two different civilizations. If we attempt to compare the world's earliest towns we can see that at the same period of time very different and diverse human habitations appeared and existed side by side.

Cities in the Middle Ages

Encounters with the civilization of a distant continent were not the only surprises. European towns of the Middle Ages had also experienced changes which distanced them further from the knowledge of Roman builders than an ocean voyage might have done.

The Middle Ages replaced the Ancient World chronologically, so one might expect that they drew on the knowledge gathered by the Romans. However, the new era's beginnings were marked by large-scale devastation and destruction. European towns which formerly had many thousands of inhabitants shrunk to settlements of several hundred people. The exceptions were the maritime trading centres, Venice in the south and Bruges to the north. The situation outside medieval Europe was different. Byzantine towns grew larger and richer, especially

A medieval town with a cathedral under construction, which took much longer than one man's lifetime. The demarcation of town walls and the foundations of the cathedral were established at approximately the same time. Soon the walls securely embraced the town which became crowded with medieval buildings, whose height and also construction material changed in time. However, the building of the cathedral, around which the town originally grew up, continued, and the completed building was the result of many generations' work.

The spread of Venice on a marshland lagoon between the 7th and 16th centuries. Venice was one of the most important cities of the world, as well as one of the trading and artistic centres. Its development is unique in many aspects. It covers more than one hundred small islands, which are situated in the middle of a huge lagoon interconnected by canals. At first, isolated settlements appeared on individual islands. Their inhabitants sought refuge there from invading tribes of Goths and Huns. They used wooden stakes to stabilize the marshland soil. They built their houses in places where no one else would expect to find human habitats, and constructed navigation routes throughout the islands. In the 7th century the individual settlements merged and from then onwards a powerful city state, with a successful merchant fleet, developed in the lagoon.

Wooden poles stuck in the bottom of the lagoon have borne the foundations of splendid Venetian palaces until the present day.

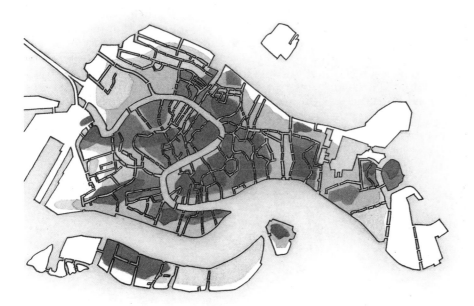

Stabilized and inhabited areas

until the 7th century   until the 9th century   until the 12th century   until the 16th century

A *veduta*, an extremely accurate and detailed drawing of Venice on one of the maps of the world published towards the end of the 17th century. It depicts the city at its zenith: a galley surrounded by gondolas sets sail from St. Mark's Square. This heralds the beginning of a ceremony celebrating the sea and Venice's dominion over it. The picture points to the position of the Venetian Republic at that time and to the sources of its fame and power.

Constantinople and towns under Islamic rule such as the imposing Baghdad in Mesopotamia or Samarkand in central Asia. In addition, Kiev and Novgorod also became important political and trading centres.

The first millennium was a troubled time of power struggles, population migration and the re-settlement of populous barbaric tribes and nations throughout the European territory. It took until the beginning of the second millennium for the new inhabitants, who arrived from harsher climates, to settle and start cultivating land and raising domestic animals. The primitive agriculture of early feudalism could not even feed those who worked on the land, let alone any urban inhabitants. However, an effective production cycle, familiar from urban civilizations thousands of years old, began to recur from the 12th century. Farmers began to increase their yields using more advanced iron technology and harnessing domestic animals. Agricultural surpluses provided food for those in other occupations, especially craftsmen. They, in their turn, produced new types of tools and implements for the farmers. Bartering contributed to the spread of common currencies and trade. Furthermore, the need to provide foodstuffs led to colonisation of virgin soil. Towns became centres of colonised regions, with their craft basis, as they already were in traditional agricultural areas.

Human habitats in medieval

Information about the life and development of towns was gathered and collated by Dutch cartographers towards the end of the 16th century and in the 17th century. They printed plans, maps and atlases which depicted the new appearance of the world. Their masterpieces were *vedutas* of famous cities.

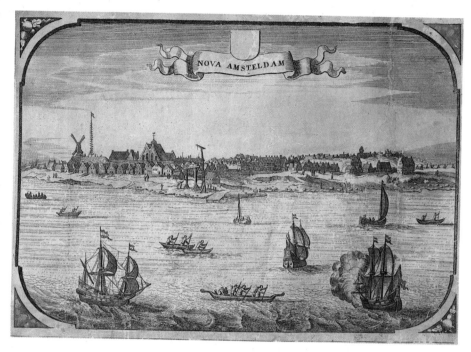

New Amsterdam (New York) on a map of America dating from *c.* 1646.

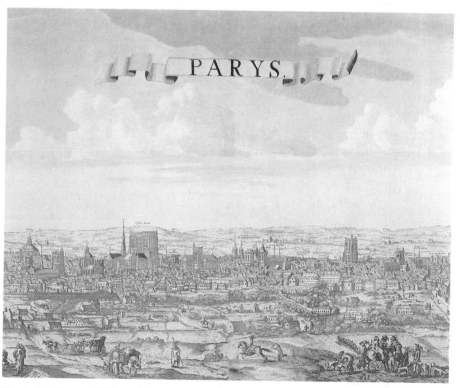

Paris in the middle of the 17th century.

Europe probably developed in three ways. Firstly, towns grew up on the ruins of ancient towns if the new social conditions permitted. Their siting in agricultural areas and at the crossroads of traditional trade routes was highly advantageous. This was true of Rome (however, its population was significantly smaller in the Middle Ages) and furthermore independent fortified estates appeared within the area of the classical metropolis), Paris (Lutetia), London (Londinium), Budapest (Aquincum), Vienna (Vindobona) and many other towns or former military garrisons in the former Roman provinces.

The second and the most typical group were the towns which grew up in close proximity to, or from the foundations of, older settlements; often adjacent to monasteries or beside castles which might provide protection in perilous times. In addition these sites were often also convenient for river crossings; or were at the crossroads of important trade routes. Traders' settlements with their houses and warehouses grew up around a central marketplace (which gradually achieved the appearance of a modern square). The streets, filled with artisans' workshops and burghers' houses, were built roughly parallel with the former trade routes. These market settlements very soon became the natural economic, administrative and cultural centres for neighbouring villages and farm estates. The majority of European towns grew grad-

London in the 1690s.

Prague in the first half of the 17th century.

ually on an irregular ground-plan out of these settlements. Thus, the towns were, in fact, established much earlier than is stated in their founding charters, which are nowadays so carefully kept in municipal archives.

The third group, also quite numerous, consisted of newly founded, colonised towns. Kings and rulers, but also the

60

It is a common assumption that the size of town buildings continuously increases. However, development is not always uncompromisingly straightforward. Let us compare the grandiose town areas and buildings of ancient cities with what replaced them many centuries later. Looking at the town plan of one residential quarter of Florence, we can easily guess where the Roman amphitheatre was situated. It was not as large as the Colosseum in Rome, but dozens of houses were built on its circular ground-plan which was criss-crossed by two streets.

Stone masonry of ancient buildings, the ruins of which have been studied by generations of architects.

Opus reticulatum

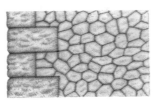

Opus incertum

Opus incertum (with corner stones)

Quadratum

Isodomon

Pseudoisodomon

nobility and, possibly, the Church initiated their foundation. People skilled in art and the builder's craft were invited from abroad or from more advanced regions. Town colonisation contributed to the development of production, trade, agriculture and the intermingling of customs and cultures. These towns also strengthened their rulers' influence in more distant regions. For example in France, King Louis IX (1226—1270) founded many towns, the so-called bastides, to strengthen his authority; in England, Edward I (1272—1307) was responsible for the foundation of many towns; the city of Venice founded its satellite towns, such as Bern, in what is now Switzerland; German towns, such as Greifswald, also fall into this category.

Colonized towns were the most significant urban tendency of the Middle Ages. Several

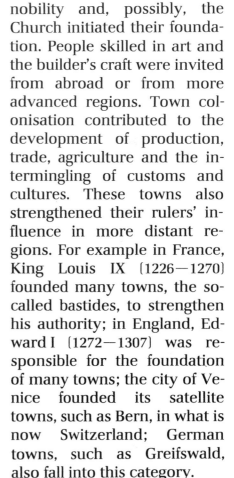

► Narrow medieval building lots merged in the course of further building development. Houses of different proportions appeared on these new sites. They had a variety of façades; the shape of windows altered, as well as the details of entrance doors; the arrangement of ground floor shop-windows was influenced by fashion and by a changing lifestyle, in addition to contemporary construction crafts.

Building development of a typical central European town. It was often established near a river, close to a ford, where merchants stopped, or at a crossroads where in time a settlement with a market place appeared. The ford became inefficient and was replaced by a bridge; after the first bridge a bridge was built. The town spread gradually and its growth continues.

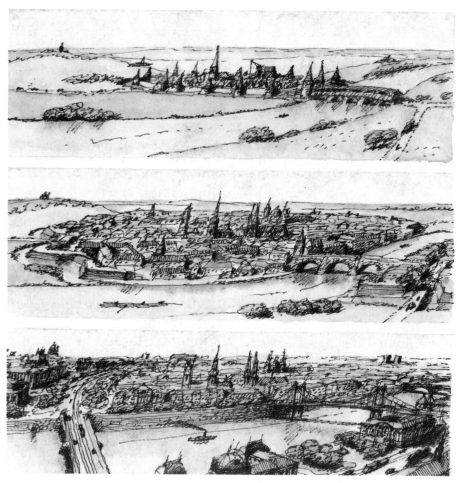

hundred of these were founded in Europe in the 13th century. People entrusted with the foundation of towns, the so-called 'locatores', were experienced in creating new environments. Regular squares with their network of streets were typical compared to the irregularly shaped settlements which grew unplanned. The 'locatores' also paid attention to the provision of drinking water and proper fortifications. However, these provisions (sewage system,

Typical church façades throughout the centuries highlighting the
different architectural styles:
Greek temple, Roman temple,
Early Christian basilica, Roman-
esque church, Gothic church,
Renaissance church, Baroque
church, Classicist church and
a church from the latter half of the
20th century.

water supplies, hardened
streets) in medieval towns
were of a lower standard than
those found in many ancient
cities.

Medieval towns, if not damaged by more modern con-
struction work, have pre-
served their unique atmosphere until now. They are varied and picturesque. They are
also noteworthy for their
builders' relationship to the
site itself, its history and natural features. Streets by-passed
rocky promontories, bogs and
streams as this facilitated contemporary traffic and provided for the most economic
construction. It would have
been unnecessarily demanding and expensive to level the
original terrain. We can also
discover in the original
ground plan of the newly
founded towns places with
which people had established
a special relationship over entire generations. For example,
the siting of some buildings,
such as churches and market
squares and street directions
have remained as a lingering
memory. These traditions
proved so strong that the new
builders were willing to
change their original plans ac-
cordingly.

These were towns for ped-
estrians and this was reflected

in their size; the width and length of their streets and squares; the relatively large number of rather narrow house façades, which had shops and little workshops on the ground floor. The scale of medieval historical centres was rather similar to our concept of pedestrian zones in modern town centres. They are in contrast to the wide, straight motorways with fly-overs and complex junctions which can lead cars fast and safely through the city but would be much less pleasant for the pedestrians.

A Return to Ancient Times

The fall of the Roman Empire in the 5th century A.D. was followed, as previously mentioned, by the decline of Rome, which lasted many centuries. Many other towns also became depopulated. It was only in the 15th century that the Renaissance revived an interest in classical art and literature. Medieval builders, too, looked to the classical era for inspiration and technical expertise. The remains of Roman structures became the template of architectural styles and designs. Leon Battista Alberti, a Florentine architect, writer, painter and musician, wrote his *Ten Books on Architecture*, inspired by classical literature and the building skills of the Greeks and Romans. Other architects also wrote theoretical treatises on urban architecture.

The best Italian artists gathered once again in Rome during the flourishing Renais-

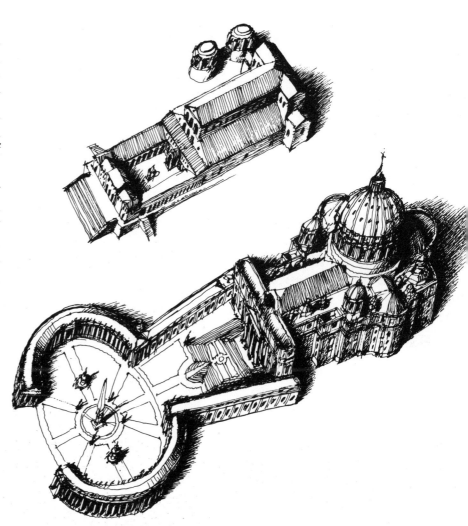

Rome, St. Peter's Square: the development of one of the best known urban space in Europe. The top drawing depicts the area at the beginning of the 16th century. It then changed into the grandiose Baroque composition which was completed in the 1660s, when a colonnade designed by Gian Lorenzo Bernini was erected.

A look inside the Renaissance palace of the Medici family in Florence.

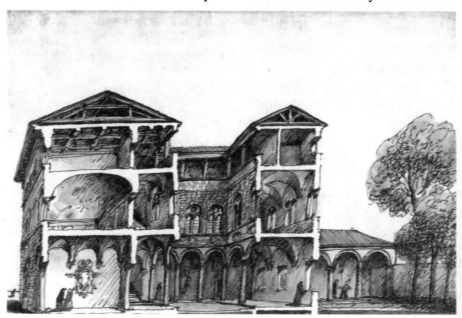

sance at the beginning of the 16th century, notably Bramante Donato, Raphael (Raffaello Sanzio), Michelangelo (Michelangelo Buonarroti) and Antonio de Sangallo. They were an entire generation of architects who began the remarkable reconstruction of the Holy City. The newly elected Pope Sixtus V (1585) desired that Rome must reflect the increasing power and wealth of the Catholic Church.

His urban intentions were also reflected in the Vatican Library fresco, which depicted the city of Rome as a network of wide streets and churches. This new urban design was further enhanced by the more dynamic and ceremonial Baroque and later, in altered form, by Classicism at the end of the 18th century. Classical architecture influenced and affected the construction of new buildings in Rome and throughout the rest of Europe for hundreds of years, although with different features in different periods.

This influence is visible in window frames and ledges, in the portals of entrance gates and in the design of important municipal areas. Builders themselves learnt a great deal through observing carefully ancient ruins, appreciating them as if they were discovering a whole new world.

The street acts as a stage for urban life. In the 16th century Sebastiano Serlio, inspired by Vitruvius's *Ten Books on Architecture*, created a collection of theatrical settings. These three scenes — *Scena Rustica*, also called *Satirica*, *Scena Gotica*, or *Comica*, and *Scena Classica*, or *Tragica* — are not merely a survey of architectural styles but give expression to various aspects of the world and depict its fortunes. (Here you can see the second and third scenes.)

Four centuries later, in the 1980s, another vision was added to those historical settings during the Venice Architecture Bienniale. Denis Crompton, an architect, composed a post-modern scene using contemporary designs exhibited there. Rather sardonically he called in *In the Shadow of Serlio*.

In Addition

Let us try to imagine what a town would look like if it were built at varying times employing different approaches but built in the same location and setting.

One example might be the medieval construction. Initially buildings were low and wooden, but later stone buildings became more common. These reflected local conditions — streets followed the direction of established routes and terrain. We can observe how the town grew around the original marketplace. However, medieval builders worked to a certain pattern. In most cases, the ground plan of a square and the size of individual building lots were strictly determined in advance.

Another example seems, at first sight, to be a town built in a completely different setting.

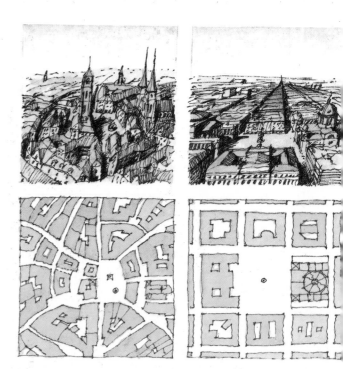

Approaches to the founding of towns — different scales; different views on the role which town quarters should play in the life of the settlement; different appreciation of areas created at random, or sometimes created deliberately.

We can see that the terrain was partially levelled by man. The rectangular ground-plan of living quarters and streets, which was a typical feature of this form, was based on a unified urban plan. This design not only complied with changed views on what a town should look like but also enabled faster construction. The builders attempted to overcome a certain monotony resulting from austere planning by using more varied and brighter façades for buildings; by emphasizing the corners of houses at crossroads; and by building architecturally dominant structures which catch our attention and give us a sense of direction.

The appearance of towns is affected both by the manner of their foundation together with the development of architectural styles and by the technical and technological skills of builders and the resources available. As towns grew and their populations increased, the

scale of private and public houses also increased. The original small wooden houses were replaced by larger buildings constructed of stone or bricks. One reason might also have been an attempt to protect towns from the hazard of fire.

As time went by, iron structures and later steel structures began to appear. In particular these new technologies have been employed

in the construction of high-rise buildings since the end of the 19th century. Human habitats have acquired another dimension, they have grown upwards. The three hundred metre high steel tower, designed in 1889 by A.G. Eiffel for Paris, symbolizes the beginning of high-rise constructions. It was, however, Chicago which became the pioneer of high-rise buildings several years before the construc-

Construction materials used by the builders of residential buildings affect their stability, their length of life and the possibilities of shaping the external appearance of the structure: timber buildings, clay buildings (from adobe); architecture emphasizing the brickwork; dwellings made of stone; the architecture of steel constructions; present-day architecture based on concrete.

tion of the Eiffel Tower. After a disastrous fire in 1871, multi-storey buildings were built, which were the predecessors of modern skyscrapers. New York soon surpassed Chicago in the number and height of its buildings. The modern city of New York was determined by land prices. The expensive building lots on Manhattan island contributed to the appearance of its very typical panorama of concentrated high-rise skyscrapers.

Financial considerations and aspects of scale and time have become important when constructing towns. New buildings and entire towns can no longer be constructed over decades or centuries as medieval cathedrals were. A well-executed detail of craftsmanship is no longer so vital. The latest technologies, whether using steel, reinforced concrete or precast structures, enable us to build human habitats in a very short period of time like an assembly line. However, the functional and utilitarian aspects of a building are often emphasized to the detriment of its aesthetic value.

68

A Guide to the Historical Labyrinth

c. 750 —According to some archaeologists the fall of Teotihuacán — a remarkable urban civilization in Mexico. The beginning of the Teotihuacán culture, its Pre-Classical period, dates from the 6th century B.C. This town of temples and priests, on a symmetrical ground-plan, reached its zenith between the 5th and 7th centuries A.D. (its population was estimated at 125,000—200,000 inhabitants).

762 — Baghdad, the biggest metropolis of the 8th and 9th centuries A.D., the seat of Caliphs and the centre of world trade and Islamic art, was founded at the site of the oldest habitation on the River Tigris. The city's atmosphere is depicted in The Arabian Nights, *also known as 'One Thousand and One Nights'.*

768—814 — Aachen, the seat of the Franconian King Charlemagne, built on the site of a Roman spa, was the first medieval European metropolis and became the model for many European cities.

The Mayan Empire stretched across the Yucatán Peninsula, modern Guatemala and Belize, parts of the Mexican states of Tabasco and Chiapas, and the western parts of Honduras and El Salvador. Some scientists argue that one of the reasons for the decline of this important and widespread civilization was the excessively intensive farming around their cities, which completely exhausted the soil. Densely populated cities were abandoned when food supplies were unobtainable. This may well have been true in the case of Tikal, whose magnificent ruins indicate the grandeur of Mayan settlements.

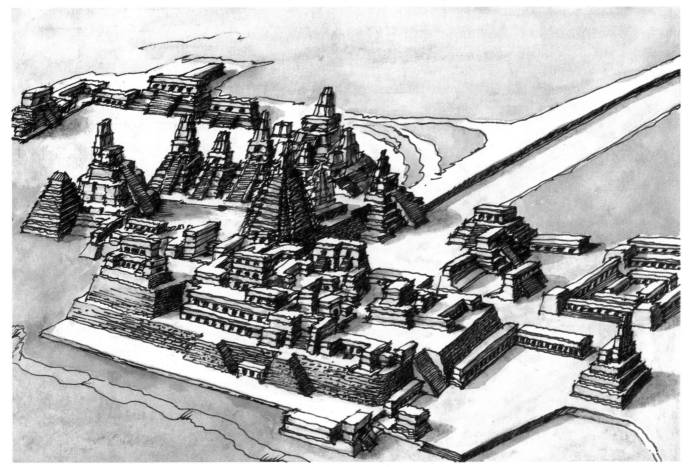

9th century — Kiev became the capital of Muscovite Russia.

889 — The last decorated stone stele was positioned on the great square of Tikal, the largest Mayan city in modern Guatemala, in Central America. Soon afterwards Tikal was abandoned, like the majority of Mayan towns, and became overgrown by virgin forest. The Mayans did not create a unified state but established city states. The Mayan cities reached their zenith in the so-called Classical Period [the Old Empire] between A.D. 250 and 900.

10th century — The rise of settlements in central Europe, which represented a transitory stage to the medieval town.

12th—13th century — Angkor Thom, the capital of the Khmer kingdom, reached the zenith of its power. It had about one million inhabitants and became an important centre of learning in South-East Asia; it was abandoned in 1432 and became overgrown by the jungle.

1212 — Genghis Khan [1155—1227], the founder of the Mongol Empire, conquered and destroyed Peking; he and his successors' armies devastated hundreds of towns during their raids.

1240 — The Tartars conquered Kiev, and a year later they reached Hungary and occupied the town of Buda.

1241 — The northern German towns of Lübeck and Hamburg created a league in order to protect their commercial interests in the North Sea and the Baltic Sea; the beginning of the Hanseatic League of Germanic towns, which made a substantial contribution to the development of medieval towns in northern Europe; this League guaranteed their economic prosperity and political independence.

1293 — The city of Florence adopted a new constitution, 'Ordinamenti di Giustizia', which laid down the pre-conditions for its economic, social and cultural development.

1296 — The English King Edward I [1239—1307] summoned 'locatores' to discuss the establishment of new towns.

1298 — Marco Polo, the Venetian explorer, dictated in prison an account of his experiences, later called Il Milione, which is the best source of knowledge concerning the 13th century Asian cities.

1325 — The Aztec city Tenochtitlán began to expand in the middle of Lake Texcoco in Mexico; the Aztecs' empire was destroyed between 1519 and 1521 by the Spanish conquistadores.

1333 — The Emperor Charles IV, King of Bohemia and Holy Roman Emperor, founded the fortified town of Monte Carlo in Italy.

15th century — Moscow became the capital of a centralized Russia.

1485 — Leon Battista Alberti [1404—72] published his Ten Books on Architecture [De re aedificatoria], *the fundamental theoretical work on Renaissance architecture and urban planning.*

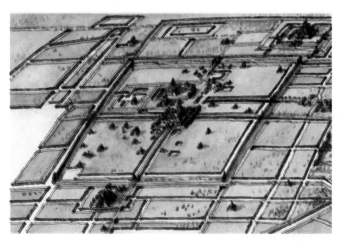

Angkor Thom, the city of a civilization based on water. Its structure was determined by religious faith and practical demands. The jungle-covered ruins made it possible to reconstruct the appearance of the extinct city, with its network of canals.

IV *A Gateway into the Hidden World of the City*

When we enter the square it is as if we were walking onto a stage. Hundreds of dramas are enfolding simultaneously. The varied façades of houses form a colourful background to these performances. The cities have to be alive to function, they must have their inhabitants with their lives, or they ultimately end up as archaeological sites.

So what are the conditions for the city to exist as a living entity?

The answer to this question lies in the hidden world of the city, behind the diverse and colourful façades of its houses. Visitors do not usually see this, but it is the hidden systems which truly determine the functioning of growing human habitats — systems such as the sewage system, the water supplies, power and energy, and other essential services as the population increases. The city's layout resembles a living organism with its life-sustaining arteries, its stomach, brain and nervous system. All of these are delicate, easily damaged and in constant need of care and maintenance. Any neglect might lead to a catastrophe.

The Sewage System in Ancient Times

In this regard Mohenjo-daro occupies an exceptional place in the mozaic of ancient settlements. Its solution to the sewage problems facing any large settlement of people was extremely advanced. The inhabitants of Mohenjo-daro created a combined sewage and water supply system. Each house usually had its own well and the dwellings were equipped with bathrooms and something approaching modern flush lavatories. This was both hygienic and necessary in the local climate.

Each dwelling was connected to the town's sewage system by a ceramic pipe which passed through its wall. Major impurities were trapped in basins out in the streets while the effluent was led away in brick channels which were covered with stone slabs or burnt bricks. We cannot but admire the ancient builders' foresight and the consistency

with which they tackled this task. In order to appreciate more fully how advanced they were for their time we might recall that at the beginning of the 20th century, a thousand years later, sewage flowed in uncovered ditches through the streets of many European towns and cities. And even now there are no sewage systems in some of the overcrowded metropolises of the developing countries. In the Brazilian cities of São Paulo and Rio de Janeiro, a third of the inhabitants do not have direct supplies of drinking water; millions of inhabitants drink water which is unhygienic and polluted by sewage.

The two issues are linked. It is necessary to provide both sufficient quantities of drinking water and to dispose of sewage safely in densely populated cities. Otherwise there is a danger of the spread of disease and epidemics.

The needs and requirements of modern city inhabitants could not be satisfied by private wells and sludge pits with septic tanks. Thus, an efficient water supply and sewage treatment plants are the most vital but also the most expensive structures in the hidden world of the city. They are linked to the city through a network of water mains and sewers which run to many kilometres in length.

The Cloaca Maxima

What has survived from the past in modern towns? Is it merely the architectural glories and monuments eulogized in tourist guides?

Once again we return to Rome. Its example shows that important technical or purely utilitarian structures might play a key role in further urban development or might even determine the shape and use of entire areas of the city in the decades, centuries or even millenniums to come.

Rome's history starts with wooden sheds, called 'tuguria'. They stood on the Palatine Hill, one of the seven hills of Rome, rising above the marshy land on the left bank of the River Tiber.

At the beginning of the first millennium B.C. the settlement on the Palatine Hill was home to the Latini, one of numerous tribes settled in the area. Later, settlements ap-

The inconspicuous exit of a technical structure may be more significant to the efficient functioning of a city than all the magnificent buildings above it. The Cloaca Maxima constructed by the builders of ancient Rome is depicted in a guidebook illustration from the 1880s, when it was still untouched by modern construction activity.

The Baths of Caracalla in Rome. A glimpse of the largest public spa in Rome.

peared on other hills. Their communication was restricted by marshland. However, the Etruscans, who began to arrive in the western part of central Italy from the 8th century B.C., influenced the course of further settlement. They were one of the most advanced ancient civilizations, with considerable building skills. They built an ingenious technical structure—a canal to drain the marshland. This canal was later used as a huge sewer (the Cloaca Maxima), and became the basis of Rome's sewage system. It has been operational ever since.

The drained area became a convenient centre of communal and commercial life. The hill inhabitants were drawn to it naturally. It was at

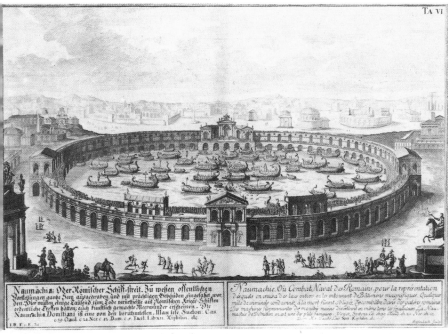

Naumachia, a huge water reservoir for games which resembled sea battles. The Emperor Augustus had it built on the right bank of the Tiber in the year 2 B.C. Many technical obstacles had to be overcome in order that town people could be entertained. The reservoir, which was more than 500 metres long and 350 metres wide, had to be filled with water. The builders constructed a new pipeline from a lake which was situated 30 kilometres away. It was a unique structure in the history of cities. This engraving itself is an imaginary reconstruction by the Austrian architect J. B. Fischer von Erlach (1656—1723) for his *History of Architecture.*

Pont du Gard near Nîmes, France: an aqueduct carrying water built above a viaduct carrying road traffic. This is a technical structure from the 1st century A.D. which is still in use. Roman carriages have been replaced by motor-cars.

the crossroads of their routes where they assembled, traded and attended social functions. The drainage canal, which was primarily a utilitarian structure, took on tremendous social importance and was a determining factor in the establishment of a new city there. The Romans themselves endowed their future settlements with what they had known as their birthright: they paid attention primarily to the hidden world of technical amenities such as drainage and sewage systems, water mains, baths, roads and fortifications.

We can simultaneously observe how certain historical decisions, whose consequences have survived for generations, affected the future appearance of the city. Communal life blossomed for centuries on that drained area. The famous Forum Romanum was established there. The imposing Roman street the Via Sacra passed through and has remained an important urban axis along which the city later developed.

In later years, the Romans did not lay emphasis on the building merely of palaces, temples and assembly areas. For example, ships landed at an expensively built port; the stone bridge, 'Pons Aemilius', was built over the Tiber in the 2nd century B.C.; important streets were paved. In the 4th century B.C. Rome was surrounded by stronger walls; gradually the sophisticated structures of aqueducts appeared, bringing water from distant springs. Appius Claudi-

Cities are not static and motionless. They live through the lifestyle of their inhabitants. They are the stage for a permanent fashion show which presents arrays of colours, materials, new clothing, new designs and various decorative accessories. Each period presents different opportunities and different goals. It is true that, superficially, a lifestyle is represented by a masquarade of costumes, but, at a deeper level, lifestyles revolve around both existing and new activities, around a variety of constantly changing pastimes and the reassessment of values and ideas. The clothing—like town architecture—mirrors the everyday life of the period. However, people replace their clothing several times during their lifetime; each generation wears different styles of clothing, although they continue to live in an environment which may well remain unchanged for centuries.

us built the earliest aqueduct in 312 B.C. This provident magistrate was also responsible for the construction of the Via Appia (the Appian Way) which ran from Rome to Capua. He realized the importance of road communications for the development of settlements.

'Your name signified it itself, oh Rome, that you shall rule over many lands', says the poet Tibullus in one of his elegies. This line expresses the mood of the period which was filled with military expeditions, quarrels and internal disturbances. It also shows that the technical knowledge concerning urban development did not necessarily spread by peaceful means throughout Europe.

The Roman Emperors and contemporary builders understood what was needed for the proper functioning of a vast and populous city. In addition to caring about food supplies, hygiene, street cleanliness and security, they also appreciated the need to provide culture and amusements for the urban inhabitants. This was the reason for erecting many public buildings and structures for education and leisure.

Marketplaces provided bodily nourishment, whereas food for the mind could be found in theatres (e.g. the Theatre of Marcellus); open-air stone amphitheatres (the Colosseum in

Rome, which held fifty thousand spectators, was the most famous); huge reservoirs for water sports surrounded by tiered seats (the so-called 'naumachia'); and circuses (Rome's Circus Maximus enabled up to 385,000 spectators to watch horse racing).

Baths, too, were common meeting places, although we might now consider them unusual. The baths were technically complex structures but they greatly improved health and morale among the citizens. They usually consisted of a spacious complex of heated buildings with running hot and cold water. Visitors took different baths; they walked from roofed rooms to spaces reserved for games and sports; public orations and closed circle debates also took place there. The baths were so popular that in the 2nd century A.D. there were one hundred and seventy of them; in the 4th century nearly a thousand. The Bath of Caracalla, the largest bath in Rome, could cater for three thousand citizens simultaneously, and it was free of charge.

Rome is said to have had at that time more than 46,600 tenement houses, 1,790 palaces, and 144 public lavatories which were intended to improve hygiene in the densely populated ancient city. A special governor (Praefectus Annonae) supervised the food supplies; the city had 290 warehouses; the cabbage marketplace (Forum Holitorium), which was reserved for the sale of groceries and vegetables; and over 250 bakeries which baked bread for the city of Rome.

In or Out of Sight?

What are the ground rules for separating or dividing up a city? What should be considered important and, conversely, what should remain out of sight?

This question is often asked by contemporary builders as well as their predecessors. It is true that not everything that looks magnificent and imposing is necessarily the most important. We have to apply both aesthetic and utilitarian criteria.

Leon Battista Alberti, the Italian Renaissance architect and Florentine artist, attempted to combine these two apparently opposing approaches: 'The beauty of the city will be greatly enhanced if various artisan workshops are built in the city districts and areas appropriate for them. There will be bankers, painters and goldsmiths around the square; nearby them shops with aromatic spices and merchandise, tailor shops and those which are considered important. Ugly merchandise should be secluded in more distant places.'

He also stresses logistical and what we now call ecological reasons. Every kind of human activity is linked to the surrounding environment and leaves its marks on it, often negative ones, such as soil or air pollution. Alberti discovered what we would call nowadays 'a functional division of town areas'. These functions have to operate 'in order that everything is established and divided properly according to utility, dignity and the suitability of each object'.

Production became an important and substantial part of

The background to the life of a 17th century settlement. Suburbs on a *veduta* depicting Brussels by Dutch cartographers.

the city's hidden world. Its significance increased with the rapid change from individual craft work to large scale manufacturing. Industrial factories appeared on the outskirts of the town and led to the construction of new suburban housing in the surrounding areas, which spread rapidly and gradually encroached on the countryside at the fringes of the city. New technical discoveries and inventions, especially the more widespread use of steam power from the beginning of the 19th century, promoted further concentrations of production and settlement. These rapid changes exerted considerable influence on the shape and quality of the town environment. In addition to the main centres of Manchester, Birmingham and London, there are many other towns which could be named as examples.

Charles Dickens provides a portrait of this period in his novel *Hard Times* with a description of Coketown: 'It was a town of machinery and tall chimneys, out of which interminable serpents of smoke trailed themselves for ever and ever, and never got uncoiled. It had a black canal in it, and a river that was purple with ill smelling dye, and vast piles of building ... where the piston of the steam-engine worked monotonously up and down, like the head of an elephant in a state of Melancholy madness.'

A dirty, life-threatening and dangerous industrial town, in which industrial production overshadows everything else. A topic for a Utopian tale inspired by contemporary experience. The original illustrations by L. Benett for Jules Verne's novel *The Steel City* from the end of the 19th century.

Discovering the City's Equilibrium

Dickens' description of Coketown is just one description of a contemporary town. We can add another view of a town from those times seen from a different perspective. For a long time Paris was considered to be the unrivalled model for a modern city, remarkable not only for its vast population but also for its grandiose construction and advanced technical solutions to the functioning of its hidden world.

The magnificent reconstruction of Paris which began towards the end of 18th century had no parallel elsewhere in Europe. The two broad avenues, Champs Elysées and the Place de l'Etoile, appeared on the city's map, and later became the axis for further urban development. This development reached its peak in the 1850s under Parisian Prefect Eugène Haussmann. He authorized the construction of boulevards, up to hundred metres in width, in already built-up areas. He also established extensive parks and squares.

Haussmann and his successors earned both admiration and harsh criticism for what they had done. True, they robbed Paris of many landmarks and the intimate atmosphere of narrow streets with little houses, but on the other hand they greatly improved hygiene and living conditions as over six hundred kilometres of water mains and sewers were hid-

Town appliances which made life easier and more comfortable in the city of the late 19th and early 20th centuries.

den under the streets and pavements of Paris.

It should also be added that there were three hundred kilometres of galleries, mazes, underground passages and quarries. Building stone was excavated there from the Middle Ages up to the 19th century by the builders of palaces, churches, town houses and public works. As Paris grew bigger, its former construction facilities became part of the inner city.

The straight, wide boulevards, as envisaged by the Prefect Haussmann, were well suited to transport and they provided magnificent vistas which were often crowned with a dominant architectural feature: an important building, an obelisk, a monument or a fountain. This urban design invoked a feeling of dignity and grandeur, simultaneously promoting a sense of direction in a metropolis whose scale bore no comparison to any other contemporary city.

However, the regard for transport together with the improved hygiene and the more advanced technical facilities were not an end in themselves. The 19th century town's streets were crowded with people. It was for them, the town inhabitants, that transport had to be organized; hygiene enforced on the streets, in houses and in parks. They had to be provided with adequate supplies of water and foodstuffs, and other everyday requirements. Various services, including rubbish collection, had to be provided. When Paris was rebuilt, great care was taken by the architects to design attractive façades for houses, whose ground floors were, in turn, enlivened by shop windows and cosy cafés. Streets were lined with trees, parks were laid out, fountains were built, lanterns providing street lighting appeared and the sewer system was greatly improved. Paris became a friendly and hospitable city which overhelmed visitors with an unforgettable range of impressions and experiences.

Pulling Down City Walls

The changing 19th century cities, including their hidden worlds, were accompanied by another break from tradition. Up until this point the shape of human settlements had been influenced to a great extent by military considerations.

Towns had provided protection against enemies since the earliest times. The construction of a proper system of defensive walls was one of the most important requirements when building towns. The walls protected the town but they also limited and restricted it. Even Haussmann's grandiose plans for the transformation of Paris into a modern city took into account the encircling ring of city walls. Improved firearms and changes in the strategy and tactics of military campaigns contributed to a most significant shift in town planning and construction. Town fortifications and ringed town walls became redundant. Paris, the

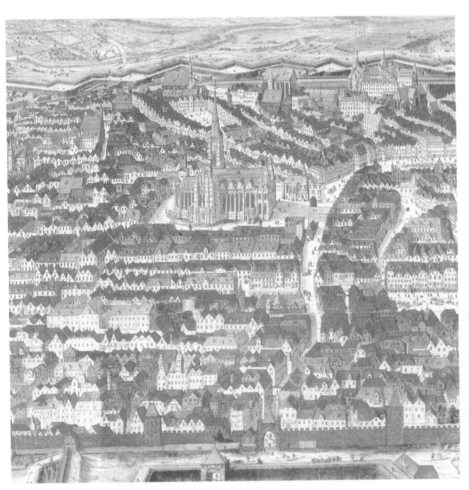

last fortified metropolis in Europe, found this out to its cost in 1871. The mighty fortifications, which were re-built many times, could not keep the Prussian armies out.

European cities, which mostly grew from medieval foundations, began to extri-cate themselves from the grip of their fortifications. New building moved beyond the area previously enclosed by fortified walls, which were now turned into urban parks, ring roads or even tenement housing.

The areas on the edge of the

A survey showing the development of central Vienna since the earliest settlement by the Romans. An outline of a Roman camp.
Fortified walls of the medieval city.
Ring road with parks and the early 19th century build-up, beyond which the town of the later 19th and 20th centuries is spreading.

◄

Vienna on a coloured *veduta* by 17th century Dutch cartographers: a fortified town encircled by walls.

former inner cities, which had been used for stabling or storehouses, were suddenly transformed into new and elegant town centres, with imposing buildings, such as the Viennese Ringstrasse.

The city's scale changed once more. It was no longer determined by redundant city fortifications. The city could expand in all directions as contemporary transport provided backup for that. Its growth also depended on the numbers of people who came to settle and work in the town.

Town planning and building began to be influenced by industrial manufacturing. Town housing employed construction units produced in larger quantities — ceiling joists and lintels, supporting beams, staircases, wash basins, water closets and artistic details for house façades.

However, the most significant aspect of this change was the emphasis on those areas beyond the former city walls.

Cities as Machines

Industrial production represented both a threat and an opportunity for the town. It polluted and damaged the environment but simultaneously it could be a means for the town's improvement and advancement. It enabled an extraordinary growth of modern technology which, in its turn, increasingly — as seen in many examples — determined the conditions of human labour. It made labour easier and provided hope for the improvement of living conditions. It is, therefore, logical that some of the planning of the Industrial Revolution towns was based on the new production efficiency concept being introduced in the factories. Only such human settlements whose individual parts each fulfilled a certain definite task, as in a well-planned working schedule, could comply with such technological conceptions. The life of urban inhabitants was almost a continuation of the working cycle.

One example of such a rational urban plan was the pro-

A perfect utilitarian construction, which has not been preserved but is much admired nowadays. An engraving of a Paris market (*Les Halles*) from 1879.

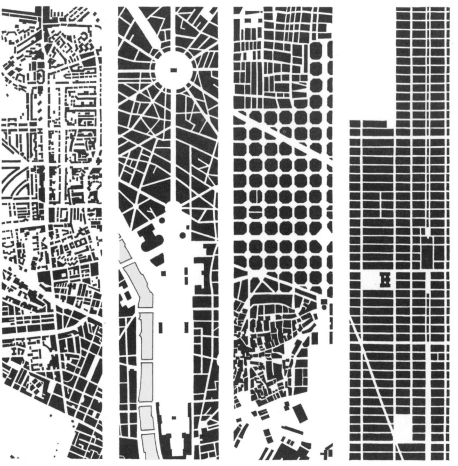

London   Paris   Barcelona   Manhattan, N.Y.

Street structures in the centres of London, Paris, Barcelona and New York illustrating different building developments and very different concepts of urban planning.

The concentration of large numbers of inhabitants in one place and the increasing scale of the city have an impact on interpersonal communication. Street posters became the most widely used form of public communication as early as the 1830s. At first they were more like notices, or written announcements. However, several decades later they sparkled with artistic vigour and colour, especially on the wide Paris boulevards. Posters revitalized the streets and became an integral part of them. Émile Zola, the French novelist, considered the street to be a most interesting modern art gallery. Examples of advertising posters evoke the atmosphere of the urban streets on which they were displayed.

ject for an ideal Industrial City (Cité Industrielle) for 35,000 inhabitants, designed in 1901—1904 by the French architect Tony Garnier (1869—1948). Garnier planned in great detail the desired structure for a modern town whose living and production quarters were separated but organically linked. In 1905 he became the City Architect of Lyon, the French industrial city, and he applied many of his theories during its expansion.

It is worth mentioning that in 1908 another famous architect, Le Corbusier (whose real name was Charles Edouard Jeanneret, 1887—1965) visited Garnier in Lyon. This meeting probably influenced Le Corbusier's subsequent urban conceptions, which — due to his exceptional creative activity — for a long time represented the benchmark for the construction and needs of modern 20th century cities. These cities were envisaged as perfectly functioning machines.

Specialist magazines and scientific journals in many countries reflected numerous and various urban conceptions in the following years. We shall, however, restrict ourselves to several schemes connected with Le Corbusier. These are considered to be among the most important in urban development.

In 1922 the 16 metre long Diorama representing a contemporary city of three million inhabitants aroused great interest at the Paris Autumnal Salon. In its central part, twenty four six-storey buildings rose around an airport. Be-

A port in an ideal city by Tony Garnier. This design attempted to encourage industrial production by facilitating transport links by rail and water. Simple, functional but comfortable housing for employees is provided around the port. Garnier advocated un- usually abundant use of reinforced concrete. In the 20th century this construction material has enabled industrialized development of human settlements on a previously unimaginable scale.

yond these, blocks of flats were dotted around, surrounded by shrubbery and greenery. This scheme surprised everyone because of its grandeur and sense of space. Two years later Le Corbusier, the Diorama's author, produced his book *Urbanisme*, which expressed great confidence in the technological civilization and its potential: 'The city is a working tool. However, contemporary towns do not usually fulfil this function. They are useless, they tire the body and corrupt the soul. They are not worthy of our era and furthermore they are no longer worthy of ourselves.'

Le Corbusier's projects directly influenced the 1928 Manifesto of important architects who joined the CIAM (Congrès Internationaux d'Architecture Moderne). It stated that urbanization represented the organization of all functions of common life in town conglomerations and in the countryside. Urbanization was not determined by aesthetic considerations but by functional requirements.

Le Corbusier was also influential in formulating the Athenian Charter which was adopted at the 4th Congress of the

A view of a contemporary city for three million inhabitants, drawn by Le Corbusier.

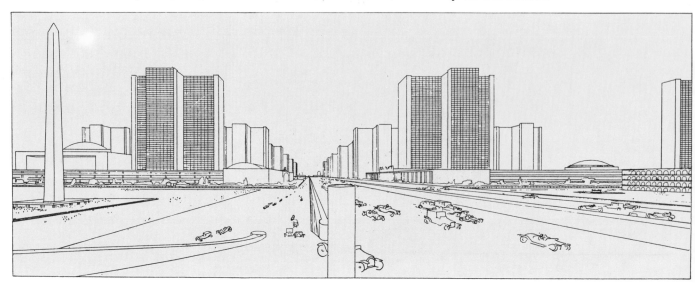

CIAM. This congress took place in the summer of 1933 on board a ship on route from Marseille to Athens and was a milestone in the development of 20th century towns. The Athenian Charter summarized the principles of a functional city divided, according to four fundamental urban functions, into zones for dwelling, working, recreation and, finally, circulation to link the three preceding functions.

Le Corbusier only realized his urban conceptions in the early 1950s when he built Chandigarh, an Indian town. Nevertheless, his town planning theories, lectures and books influenced our thinking concerning the modern city as, in addition to its appearance, he emphasized all that determines its smooth and trouble-free functioning.

Unfortunately, the results of such planning have often been disappointing. Instead of the anticipated goal of an advanced town organism functioning reliably like clockwork, new and unexpected problems have arisen. One likely explanation might be that strict functionalism proves efficient in a production line but it cannot embrace the complexity of human nature.

From Backstage to Front of Stage

Les Halles, the famous Parisian cover market, described by the French novelist Émile Zola as 'the belly of Paris', was vibrant until the middle of this century. The city's grocers met there; meat, fruit and vegetables were traded wholesale to Parisian restaurants and hotels; housewives came to shop there. However, gradually the marketplace could not keep

pace with the city. Its capacity, technical facilities and hygiene proved entirely inadequate.

This dirty hinterland became all too visible as the throbbing city centre came closer and closer to the marketplace. The bulldozers ended its existence. Only one building was left standing as a reminder of its past glories. In the 1970s the magnificent Forum des Halles, a commercial and trade centre with access to the metro system, was built on the site.

Similar developments have taken place in other large cities. However, the old factories and public works are not always destroyed. London's Covent Garden does not live on in name only; its original buildings were tastefully renovated and put to a new use. They have become a major cultural and tourist attraction.

A city's backstage ages fast. It requires continuous main-

The refuse of a modern city includes kitchen left-overs, the packaging from various goods, cans, plastic bags and bottles and also broken TV sets and rusting car bodies. Industrial and technological structures which are being phased out or have already been decommissioned represent a special kind of refuse, as do warehouses and factories which are no longer in use. The lifespan of structures which facilitate the smooth functioning of the town is usually quite limited. However, it is possible to recycle and re-use some of the refuse.

tenance. The parameters of public works change; in time the buildings deteriorate; their capacity becomes inadequate; they stand on land whose value soars as the city centre encroaches on it.

Individual streets and districts of a city acquire not only their names but also their specific character due to certain products having been produced there for years. These formerly overlooked and hidden places become fashionable and are utilized once again. One example is the former dockland area of London which became a huge building site in the 1980s. For hundreds of years ships had docked there, loading and unloading goods from all over the world which were stored in warehouses close to the centre of London. It appears as if a new town has been built on the site. However, several preserved and renovated warehouses, a pumping station for the London power station, a mill and scattered workshops remain. They are the only fragments of the past which have survived extensive slum clearance. They continue to reflect the irreplaceable flavour of 19th century London.

The economic backstage where the smell of fish mixed with the scent of imported spices: Gustave Doré's *London Dockyards* in the 19th century.

In Addition

What is to be done with refuse? Where is it to be put or hidden; where can it be dumped?

These are not new questions. They were already being asked by the inhabitants of the earliest town settlements. We know that the first notice banning the dumping of rubbish in the streets dates from around 500 B.C. This happened in Athens whose inhabitants set up town rubbish dumps. These had to be situated at least one mile beyond the city walls.

Unfortunately, medieval European towns lost sight of the many Greek archievements

It appeared that the question of refuse had been finally resolved when a special collection service to carry away rubbish was introduced in towns. Rubbish was removed beyond the town walls. However, as the towns grew, new buildings encroached on these rubbish dumps. There were fewer sites where it was possible to dump rubbish and again the recurring question was how to dispose of it.

In 1874 the first attempt was made to burn refuse in Nottingham, England. Ever since, special incinerators have been built, especially near densely populated areas. Refuse works

The landscape of rubbish.

which contributed to a cleaner and healthier urban environment. For example, the Parisians threw their rubbish out of the windows onto the street until the 14th century. And even several centuries later when people were moving in search of work to new industrial centres, which were rapidly growing into large cities, the question of refuse disposal was usually 'resolved in a simple manner'. The streets of industrial outskirts were bordered by heaps of refuse, while ditches alongside the roads carried away sewage and water from households.

are another specific feature of the hidden world of the city. At present, about 90 per cent of all refuse in American cities is incinerated. New York's inhabitants dispose of or throw out nearly 24,000 tonnes of refuse daily.

However, not all refuse is suitable for incineration. Many experts attempt to devise new ways of utilising refuse; recycling it as opposed to destroying it. The hidden world of the town is now equipped with bottle banks, paper banks and other recycling facilities which enable the re-use of glass, paper and metals for industrial processing.

A Guide to the Historical Labyrinth

1516 — Thomas More published his Utopia.

1533 — Cuzco, the capital of the Incas in Peru, was conquered by the Spanish. Tradition has it that it was founded by the legendary Manco Capac c. A. D. 1000; it reached its peak in the 15th century. The Incas founded many other planned towns, such as Ayaviri, Pisco, Ollantaytambo, Machu Picchu, which became the last refuge of the Incas fleeting from the conquistadores.

1565 — Amsterdam (formerly a fishing village which grew into one of the most important maritime and academic centres of the 16th and 17th centuries) adopted a building code. It was a unique example of a successful regulation for a rapidly developing city which in following years was connected and also characterized by its network of canals (grachten).

1580—1588 — The construction of Nové Zámky in Slovakia, a star-shaped town stronghold, which was the unique realization of an idealised Renaissance town design.

1585 — Rome became an artistic centre once more. Pope Sixtus V began the grandiose reconstruction of the Holy City.

1626 — The Dutch established New Amsterdam on territory bought from Indians. It was taken over by the English in 1664 and renamed as New York; now it is the largest city in the USA.

1661 — Louis XIV reconstructed Versailles into the most magnificent royal palace in Europe; its layout of palace buildings and gardens became the model for many later urban schemes.

1666 — The Great Fire of London destroyed 13,000 wooden houses; Sir Christopher Wren, the English architect and mathematician, planned London's reconstruction; his urban scheme was not fully realized but he designed more than fifty important London buildings.

1703 — St. Petersburg was founded.

1725 — John Wood completed his urban design which became the basis for the reconstruction of Bath, a spa town west of London; it is an example of interlinking parks with remarkable curving terraces of houses.

1755 — An earthquake virtually destroyed Lisbon; 60,0000 inhabitants died in its ruins.

1793 — A plan to establish a committee of artists to reconstruct Paris was adopted; the French Revolution prompted a new period in the construction of Paris.

1825 — Robert Owen, the English utopian socialist, founded New Harmony, an egalitarian community, in the USA.

1829 — The Galerie d'Orléans in Paris was covered with a glass cupola; however, the most famous example of a covered promenade street, which was a typical feature of 19th century urbanism, is the Gallery of Victor Emmanuel in Milan built between 1865 and 1877.

1832 — A horse-drawn street-car line opened in New York.

1851 — The first traffic interchange of roads and pedestrian paths was built in New York's Central Park long before the invention of the automobile.

1853—1870 — G. E. Haussmann was appointed Prefect of Paris; by order of Napoleon III he took charge of implementing one of the most outstanding urban reconstructions of the 19th century.

1857 — Vienna began to demolish its fortified walls and used this cleared area for building the Ringstrasse.

1863 — Housing estates for the Krupp steel works' employees at Essen were the first attempts to solve the housing problems of industrial cities.

1863 — The London Underground, the world's earliest steam-powered underground railway system, was opened.

28th January 1871 — Prussian armies conquered Paris, the last fortified metropolis in Europe.

1871 — The great fire of Chicago; burnt areas provided opportunities for new development; the first skyscraper building was erected in 1883.

1878 — The elevated railway system opened in New York.

c. 1884 — Electric tramway systems began operation in many cities (Vienna, Frankfurt-am-Main, Richmond in the USA).

1889 — The World Exhibition in Paris; the French metropolis acquired its dominant landmark: the Eiffel Tower.

1893 — The Jubilee Exhibition in Chicago grew into an extensive movement called 'The City Beautiful', led by Daniel Hudson Burnham, the Principal Architect to the Exhibition.

V A Gateway to City Inspection

A gate in fortified walls allowed entry to the city, whether on foot or by transport; the open or closed gate regulated the inhabitants' contact with the surrounding countryside.

The paths and roads which approached a gate from different directions changed within the city to streets with houses on both sides. As the city gradually grew beyond its original walls and spread to the countryside, building continued along former trading routes and military roads. Although they were adapted to new conditions, we can observe their paths in the layout of most European cities which have grown out of their medieval settlements. Many settlements appeared only because there were communications winding through the countryside. These towns grew on the sites of former marketplaces or traders' settlements; at the crossroads of trade routes; close to ports where military vessels were anchored and traders' ships landed their cargo; or at places where couriers rested and stagecoaches changed horses.

Transport between cities and on their streets is in perpetual motion, constantly circulating to achieve the movement of people, goods and merchandise. It provides a vital energy for the organism of the city. However, as the city's appearance alters, as its size increases and its population grows, the character and scale of town communications change, too. In medieval London or Paris it did not take

long to walk from one end of the city to the other. However, the contemporary size of these cities necessitates the use of bus, car or underground transport. Narrow, winding streets were suited to pedestrians provided that only the occasional horseman, burgher's coach or trader's cart passed along their unstrengthened surface. Large cities overcrowded with people and traffic require more spacious and wider streets as transport arteries which facilitate the movement and pace of traffic.

Through the Streets of Rome

The streets of ancient Rome were, in fact, the continuation of roads which approached the city from all directions. The Via Sacra, or the Holy Way, which crossed the Roman Forum, was the most outstanding and famous of these routes. It was bordered by important buildings and works of art, which provided fitting surroundings for processions and festive marches. Victorious commanders marched their troops triumphantly along its length to mark the end of successful military campaigns.

A network of narrower but busy streets and lanes was connected to the major streets. The streets of ancient Rome did not only allow for walking and transport but in fact people lived their lives there. Craftsmen worked on the pavements in front of their shops, traders offered mer-

The ruins of ancient Rome with some remaining paving on a road leading through a built-up town area. An illustration from the 1880s.

chandise for sale on the street. The areas where public life and traffic merged were paved. In some parts there was actually a raised pavement close to the houses for pedestrians.

The increase in Rome's population influenced transport; there were far more people, carts and carriages on the streets. Traffic jams were becoming unbearable and therefore traffic had to be regulated and directed. One of the first decrees of Gaius Julius Caesar, when he became Emperor, banned wheeled transport from the centre of Rome during the day.

However, this solution of the problem led to another problem. The streets became quieter and safer during the day — there were less injuries and traffic accidents — but

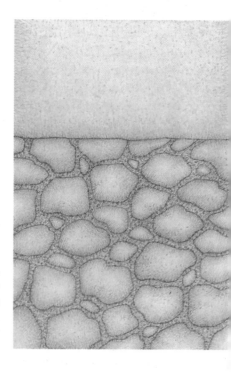

Faster modes of transport require different road surfaces. At first, gravel is replaced by stone paving which is later covered with an asphalt surface or a layer of concrete. There is one particular place on the Via Appia where the original stone road links up with the grey asphalt surface of a modern road.

correspondingly traffic increased at night. Heavy carriages rattled along the paved main streets so that it was impossible to get any sleep in the vicinity. Other restrictions

followed. For example, during the reign of Emperor Hadrian (A.D. 117—138), a decree was issued which regulated the size of loads and the number of carriages which were per-

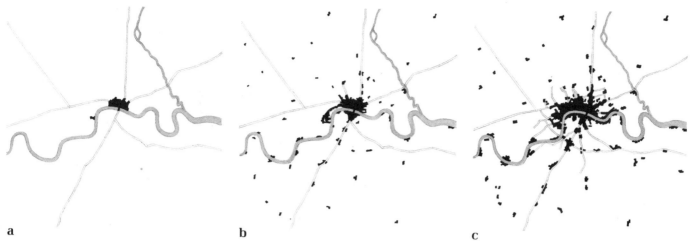

a

b

c

The importance of roads and increased traffic demands in growing cities, illustrated by London:
London during the Roman period and until approximately the end of the first millennium (a).
Medieval and Tudor London with main approach roads (b).

17th century London (c).
18th century London (d).
19th century London—the conversion of a typical European trading centre and port into a modern city, the capital of a great empire (e).
20th century London (f).

d

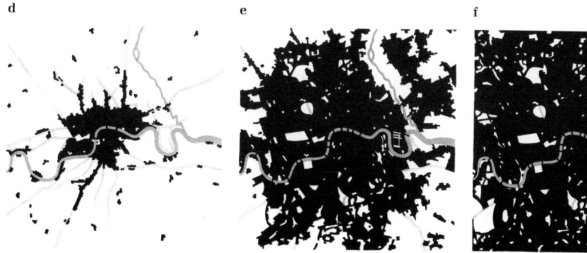

e

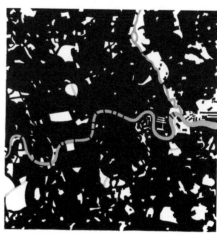

f

mitted to enter the city during both the day and the night.

Similar regulations were valid not only in Rome where the narrow side streets could not deal with traffic congestion. They were also enforced in newly founded towns designed with longer and wider streets. Ever since the earliest times it has been evident that traffic congestion cannot be solved merely by providing additional facilities for transport. Where there are fewer obstacles traffic becomes faster and more efficient, but its volume rapidly increases. Straight streets and avenues seem to attract a greater weight of traffic and a vicious circle is created.

Cities Bordering the Roads

There are arguments about what is most important when founding a town. Do we judge it by practical, sanitary or technical criteria? Or should it be primarily a question of establishing an impressive environment and a grandiose effect?

The 19th century reconstruction of Paris demonstrates that both approaches are usually involved. Unquestionably, the decisive role in determining the layout of a city is governed by transport considerations and their development. This was important long before the first automobile appeared on the streets.

Transport is so essential for

95

a city that the planning of new settlements often resembles building a complex engineering structure. In the 1880s, the so-called linear city was designed. Arturo Soria y Mata, a Spanish civil engineer, designed the town as a continuous ribbon of family houses with gardens. Its axis was a wide roadway subdivided into a carriageway, a railway, service roads and pavements. Similar linear developed towns were intended to connect historical city centres, which — due to their unsuitable communications — could not keep pace with modern times. However, only a twenty kilometre section of the entire project of a fifty kilometre city was built outside Madrid in Spain.

Urban planners occasionally return to a linear city scheme. Nevertheless, this approach does not seem to be the most favourable. Houses, factories and warehouses bordering a main thoroughfare give the impression of uncontrolled and accidental growth: their function and purpose do not seem to respect man's need to live in an aesthetically appealing and pleasing environment.

Cities Acting as Roads

The linkage of a human dwelling and a road has more than one shape. A house can also be used directly for transport, or a road may be an integral part of a dwelling; thus a road becomes a town. Residential bridges are examples from the past. That bizarre bridge, the

Residential dwellings grouped on a bridge across the River Thames in a *veduta* by Dutch cartographers.

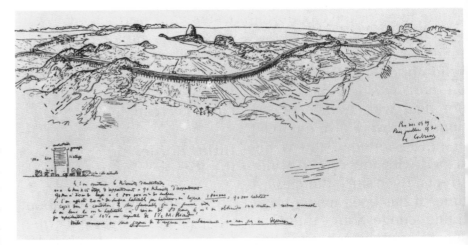

Le Corbusier's drawing of a bridge town near Rio de Janeiro: it crawls through the countryside like a snake. The overall view from the late 1920s is complemented in the bottom left corner by a more detailed design of a house whose roof functions as a road.

96

Ponte Vecchio in Florence, is often cited. It connects two opposite river banks but simultaneously has been — and still is — the home of goldsmiths. Earlier paintings also depict residential dwellings grouped on a bridge across the River Thames in the centre of London.

The 20th century has developed this historical inspiration on a gigantic scale. This corresponds to the present rapid pace of life, to the speed of traffic, to the scale of modern cities. We can quote several projects which point to the changing role of the automobile in the city despite the fact that they have not been constructed entirely as planned.

It all started in the early 1930s when Le Corbusier, one of the most famous modern architects, drove a car on the test track of the Fiat factory in the Italian town of Turin. He was most impressed with the car's speed and its technical perfection. When he shared this experience with his friends he was not yet aware that this enthusiasm for modern technology would influ-

ence and subject to the needs of the car not only the future lay-out of cities but the planning of entire regions.

The Turin test track was laid out on the roof of the Fiat factory. It seemed that the road replaced the roof of the building. Le Corbusier found this idea rational and very attractive as it saved land and construction materials too. Such a road was not an obstacle in the landscape but an important feature.

Using this idea, Le Corbusi-

er designed unconventional projects for Rio de Janeiro and Algiers. In Algiers, a continuous strip of residential houses, several kilometres long, for 180,000 workers, was to have been built. The flat roofed houses were to level the coastline terrain as a bridge and were to serve as a wide superhighway.

Nomadic Cities

When looking at similar projects an important question

Urban modes of transport through the centuries.

A city designed for cars at the end of the 20th century.

arises: If the inhabitants of modern cities are increasingly dependent on transport, will it mean they are going to spend the larger part of their lives commuting? Consequently, will tranport methods become more important than residential housing?

We can extend these thoughts further. Will cars, buses and underground trains, both individual and public transport, eventually become our mobile homes?

At first sight these ideas might look rather far-fetched. We can, however, find examples of this in the past.

The Biblical story of Noah's Ark describes man's eternal quest to find a self-supporting haven; a dwelling equipped with all that is required for survival and which will provide a refuge against the raging elements and the hostile surroundings.

A human dwelling built on fixed foundations has many advantages; in many respects, it is safer and more comfortable. However, it cannot protect the inhabitants against huge catastrophes. Neither can it survive a strong military attack. In uncertain times, a nomadic existence might be preferable. Many Asian and European towns found this to their cost in the 13th century when they were reduced to ruins by the armies of Genghis Khan, the founder of the Mongol Empire. The Mongols themselves lived in camps which resembled nomadic towns as far as their equipment and organization were concerned. They considered

Traffic congestion in a European city in the second half of the 19th century. Gustave Doré: *London Dockyards.*

fortified cities, built for permanent settlement, to be dangerous traps from which it would be impossible to escape when an enemy attacked.

What should a Nomadic city look like?

Some notions are influenced by military camps which in the past and present often have both aspects of urban and nomadic living: residential and other structures are easily assembled and transportable; their users and builders do not expect them to have a long serviceable life. There are communications, a form of streets, which often lead to a square. Living in a military camp is a provisional existence, without any involvement in the site itself. A single command, somebody's sudden decision, a change in circumstances

The future of public transport as envisaged in the 19th century.

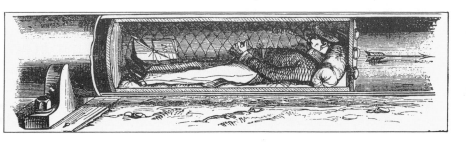

and the 'town's' existence just ends, if need be, to be resumed somewhere else, tens or hundreds of kilometres away. A similar example is gold prospecting towns; work camps and temporary settlements close to mineral deposits or huge industrial complexes, which are built far away from permanent settlements.

Hector Savinien Cyrano de Bergerac, the French philosopher, poet and eccentric, provided a pleasing image of a city which was able to move from one place to another in his fictional travelogue *A Voyages to the Moon and the Sun.* He created a human settlement which moves to a place where the weather is better: 'We have migratory or permanent cities...' explains the writer's fictional guide; 'the migratory cities are arranged in the following manner: the

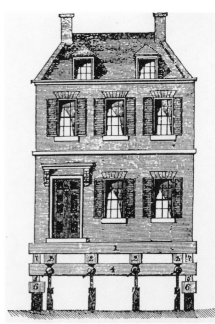

An actual house on wheels: an instruction in a technical publication from 1823 illustrating a method of moving a brick residential house to a more suitable site.

Visions of cities of several centuries: the wandering city of Cyrano de Bergerac (above) and the walking city of Ron Herron (below).

architect builds each palace, as you can see, out of a very light wood; he installs four wheels down below... when people decide to move the town somewhere else (every season it is taken where the air is different), each inhabitant unfolds a large number of wide sails on one side of his house, just adjacent to bellows. He then winds the spring which drives the bellows, and strong gusts of wind... force the houses to travel over a hundred miles in less than a week.'

Ron Herron, a member of the Archigram, a British group of architects, produced a modern equivalent of this image. His huge city walking on telescopic legs is a technical monstrosity which slowly passes through inhospitable landscapes devastated by wars; it slides through a sandy desert past the pyramids of Pharaohs; it crawls through the ruins of deserted settlements. It is a human dwelling, which, with help of the latest technology, strives to reach an unpolluted and unspoilt land.

When we look around we can see that some elements of literary and artistic imagination seem to have actually materialized. Private cars and long-distance coaches are designed and equipped so that their users are as independent as possible of their environment. In early summer, fleets of caravans appear equipped with all that is needed for modern day living — such as beds, washing facilities and a WC, a fridge and a television.

In camp sites and at the roadside temporary towns appear in which people live for weeks, months or even years in their cars and caravans. Some people find this existence cheaper while others love being mobile, unattached, independent and able to make an instant decision to move on. A town of bricks and mortar becomes a trap, an environment polluted by traffic.

People try to escape its grip but even then, how else can they achieve it other than by using transport?

Terraced Streets

A quickly drawn sketch may make a deeper impression than a fully completed house. Leonardo da Vinci (1452—

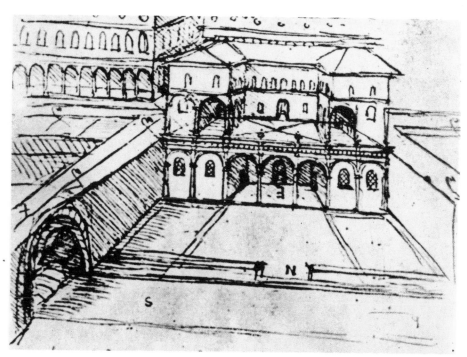

A sketch in Leonardo da Vinci's diary from 1483 to 1499 depicting a multi-level town.

A Crystal Way for London was designed by William Moseley, inspired by the opportunities by steel constructions.

1519), the Italian painter, sculptor, architect and man of science, made in his diary a sketch of a terraced street in the second half of the 15th century. This is the first known example of the multi-level regulation of transport in a city and as such is included in summaries of urban theories. Leonardo's scheme anticipated and tried to solve problems which nowadays represent the biggest headache for contemporary planners in our traffic congested cities.

Multi-level circulation of traffic has many advantages. Cars and other vehicles do not meet at crossings; they do not have to slow down; traffic flows more safely and more economically. Individual levels are adapted to different and often mutually exclusive modes of traffic, according to their character and technical specifications. For example, cars and other vehicles require a different running surface and gradient from railways; cyclists or pedestrians require differing amounts of space.

The solution to traffic problems in towns lies in the parallel development of modes of transport which use their own exclusive routes. The commentary on the cover of the magazine *Scientific American*, dating from 1913, which bore a concept illustration by Harvey W. Corbett.

In the history of urbanization, multi-level separation of various modes of transport, especially of pedestrians, has become a central feature of many elaborate town reconstruction projects or even the building of entirely new towns. In the second half of the 19th century, an Englishman, William Moseley, produced a scheme which took full account of contemporary technical possibilities. In 1855 he suggested a multi-level roadway. He called it the Crystal Way, probably named after Crystal Palace which was designed by Joseph Paxton to house the 1851 Great Exhibition at London.

In 1910, Eugène Hénard, the City Architect of Paris, submitted a project to solve this chronic malaise affecting modern cities to an international gathering of experts. He offered them his vision of 'the street of the future' and stated: 'We intend to have a street with several layers similar to our multi-storey buildings!'

A painting by Harvey W. Corbet portrays best the hope of a rapid realization of similar visions. It gives the impression that theories on the appearance of the contemporary town had a logical and ration-

Some options for alleviating traffic congestion in towns. New designs attempt to tackle the issue while preserving the traditional residential atmosphere of streets and squares. Access communications for the delivery of supplies are situated underneath a pedestrianized shopping precinct. Underground garages and car parks are situated beneath a residential block. Multi-level communications provide access to important sites in the town centre, whereas obstacles on roads which are at the same level as town streets block or at least slow down passing traffic. Another illustration depicts a road which is embedded beneath pavements for pedestrians, with foot bridges providing access to parks: traffic does not obstruct the pedestrian who can observe, from a distance, the bustle of a modern city.

It is necessary to protect the public from the ill effects of traffic by, for example, the construction of sound baffles.

al basis. However, with hindsight, this may seem rather bizarre.

What looks so simple and impressive in that painting, actually represents an extremely complex and expensive technical problem. It is difficult to estimate what is and what is not really necessary, and which direction the development of vehicles will take. It might be that an expensively created project would become obsolete at the moment of its completion. Just glance at those pictures of strange cabins, carts, moving pavements and roads for steam driven transport. They were out of date before they had served their purpose. Transport parameters change incredibly quickly. That which was designed to serve very quickly becomes a hindrance.

One result of these efforts to separate various modes of transport in many cities is, for example, underground rail and tramway networks. Pedestrian subways or foot bridges over busy streets are commonplace. Some cities have also built underground tunnels for cars and other vehicles in order to ease their passage through built-up areas.

The more imaginative projects in which a street would resemble a multi-storey building have only rarely been realized. For more than fifty years *La Défense* of Hénard's Paris has been one of the most impressive examples of a multi-layer aggregation of high rise buildings underneath which trains, roads and pedestrian routes bypass one another.

In Addition

Alone or in a crowd?

Transport in the city is an example of a means becoming an end in itself. It confirms that it is rather shortsighted to consider the movement of people in the city regardless of the environment, and only from the perspective of the maximum capacity of roads. The metropolises whose streets are designed for cars instead of people are wonderful when you are driving but not pleasant to live in.

The solution cannot be found in planning alone; in designing how a street should look, its width, or whether a route should be straight without obstacles or with turns, which would slow traffic down. The choice of transport is also important.

Discussions concerning traffic issues in the city revolve around such issues as what amount of space is to be allocated for private transport and public transport; or where movement should be restricted to pedestrians or cyclists only.

The city remains a pleasant place in which to live if an environment is created whose scale is determined by the pedestrian and where the car does not dominate. However, this becomes increasingly difficult to fulfil because there are more and more cars on the road. In the 1970s about 200 million cars were in use — in the 1990s their number has approached nearly 450 million. The majority of cars are used in towns or their surroundings. There is a conflict between the car users' interest and the public interest, or one might say the facilities which towns offer to car users.

Public transport provides a counterbalance to private cars. It has many forms and uses various kinds of vehicles. Buses and track vehicles are the most common forms of public transport.

In the streets one can see buses of various makes, shapes and sizes, from mini-buses suitable for historical towns to huge twinned, articulated buses.

Track transport in towns is represented by traditional trams and fast trains, which usually use underground tunnels (underground, tube, metro, subway) or travel above the ground, safely separated from other traffic.

Their more modern variant is the light-rail-car which travels along a reserved traffic route so that its carriages can move quickly. Suburbs and housing estates close to big cities are connected to them by fast suburban and passenger trains.

The reasons why private car journeys in town should be restricted and the public transport system improved are primarily economic and ecological. Public transport uses precious town space more effectively. Buses and trains can carry more passengers, they move faster and are safer. They require less space and, if the traffic operation is well managed, they can also save much time.

Let us, for example, consider how many people can pass through a certain place in a city using various forms of transport. When conditions are ideal, the underground can carry 70,000 passengers per hour and buses just over 30,000. In contrast, private cars, each carrying four passengers, can carry less than 8,000 people per hour.

However, not everyone is willing to give up the comfort and privacy provided by the private car. The car increases the independence of the town's inhabitant from his surroundings — it takes up more and more space. It requires new roads, better road surfaces, parking spaces. It needs regular supplies of fuel. Additionally — it has to be maintained and then replaced in time.

The only really individual form of transport in the town is walking, or perhaps cycling. It enables one to perceive and appreciate the surroundings; it provides exercise, which a person living in the town and accustomed to driving a car would otherwise undoubtedly lack. Any town which does not provide for these two forms of transport makes its inhabitants and visitors feel unwelcome and rejected.

A Guide to the Historical Labyrinth

1894 — The Spanish engineer Arturo Soria y Mata (1844—1920) founded a construction company, the Compania Madrilena de Urbanizacion, which built the first part of a 55 kilometre linear city, a new type of settlement with a tram line forming its axis.

1896 — The first Continental subway line was opened in Budapest.

1898 — Ebenezer Howard published his treatise Tomorrow: A Peaceful Path to Real Reform, which started the Garden City Movement; in 1899 the Association of Garden Cities was established.

1900 — The first part of the Metro in Paris was constructed.

1901—1904 — The French architect Tony Gar-

nier designed a scheme for an industrial city of 35,000 inhabitants, the 'Cité Industrielle'.

1902 — The first petrol-engined buses appeared on the streets of London.

1903 — The construction of the first garden town, Letchworth, England, designed by Raymond Unwin.

1906 — San Francisco, then the most important city on the American Pacific Coast, was destroyed by an earthquake and subsequent fire.

1910 — The most important town planners met in London at a conference on town construction.

1911 — A competition to design a capital for Australia, Canberra, was held and won by W. B. Griffin; the first Govern-

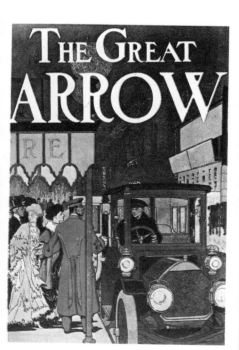

The atmosphere of the town changed with the arrival of more efficient modes of transport. Contemporary posters which appeared in the streets at the beginning of the 20th century no longer displayed impractical visions but strongly advocated the advance of elegant, modern technology.

ment offices moved to the new capital in 1927.

1913 — *The spread of the Garden City idea on the Continent led to the foundation of the International Garden Cities and Town Planning Federation.*

1914 — *The Italian architect Antonio Sant'Elia, the author of a* Manifesto of Futurist Architecture, *exhibited his projects of the futuristic city; he considered the city should 'resemble a huge humming building site, active and moving, and in a dynamic state in all its parts'.*

1919 — *Bauhaus, a school of art and architecture aiming at the integration of art and technology in design, was founded in Weimar in 1919; its professors devoted themselves to issues of modern urban construction (W. Gropius, L. Hilberseimer, H. Meyer, L. Mies van der Rohe).*

VI *A Gateway to Nature*

People also hid behind city walls in order to find protection from the natural elements. A well-built house is comfortable and safe. By building towns, mankind distanced itself from Nature. However, people return to it through this gate. They look to Nature not only as a source of nourishment but as a source of inspiration, pleasure and satisfaction.

The Story of the Corinthian Capital

At the beginning of our era Vitruvius told an unusual story in his *De architectura*. This story showed how the town dweller began to rediscover his relationship with Nature. One approach was through imitating shapes observed in Nature in the shapes and constructions of buildings erected in cities.

The Corinthian capital gave its name to the most ornate of the Greek architectural orders, which re-appeared, many centuries later, during the Renaissance period and once again in the time of Classicism. Its influence is visible in the magnificent 19th century palaces of Paris and the classically inspired buildings and post-modern buildings in American and European towns constructed towards the end of the 20th century. One example is the recent annex to London's National Gallery.

Let us return to the story that started it all. It began with an illness and the unfortunate death of a young Corinthian girl. After the funeral, her nanny gathered all the dolls which the girl used to play with in a basket. She placed the basket on her grave and covered it with a roof tile in order to protect the toys from the elements. By chance, the

The story of the Corinthian capital.

nanny put the basket on the spot where the root of an acanthus plant grew. The following spring, the root began to sprout and shoots with leaves appeared. They grew round the basket's edges and, pressed by the tile on the top, they formed spiral curves.

Then, one day, Callimachus, a sculptor famous in Athens and Greece for his delicate, noble marble works, happened to pass by the grave with its toy basket overgrown with leaves. He became interested in the unusual combination of shapes. Inspired by them he created columns for a nearby building in Corinth. These columns became the basis of the Corinthian order.

The Paradox of a Garden City

Searching for or rediscovering the urban dweller's relationship with Nature resulted primarily from practical reasons. The very quality of life in the city determined this return to Nature. This is a self-preserving tendency which usually takes place at a time when all other attempts to improve the urban life fail. The manufacture of goods concentrated in towns; their populations increased as well as the number of houses. Industrial towns at the turn of the century spread into the surrounding countryside but their housing and the density of settlement increasingly distanced them from the rural life, from Nature. The urban environment became unhealthy, unhygienic and alienated from Nature.

Towns attract new settlers but they are a mixed blessing. People crowd into them but soon begin to consider how to escape through the town gate. The question is where they can escape to while simultaneously preserving some of the advantages of urban life.

This is where the idea of garden cities originated. Its most vocal proponent was Ebenezer Howard, an English social reformer. He was a stenographer in the British House of Commons where he had heard many complaints, grievances and opinions on the ailments of 19th century towns. He summarized his views, which were strongly influenced by the Russian philosopher and geographer P. A. Kropotkin, in his 1898 book *Tomorrow: A Peaceful Path to Real Reform*. This book initiated a widespread foundation of garden cities. They were the towns which were to be different from the existing industrial centres of England, 'tumours, debilitating illnesses devouring half of a man's life'. Garden cities were to be a new type of settlement composed of clusters of family houses surrounded by gardens. They were to combine all the advantages of town and countryside life.

An Association of Garden Cities was established soon after and it founded the first settlement at Letchworth. Another example was the establishment in 1920 of Welwyn Garden City near London.

Attempts to establish garden cities took place in the majority of European countries from the beginning of the 20th century. However, the results were not always satisfactory as garden cities were not rationally designed as suggested by Howard. Instead residential districts without any linking urban design

TYPE DE L'ORDRE FRANÇOIS.

L'ORDRE FRANÇOIS DÉVELOPPÉ.

The development of an architectural order by copying or adapting shapes and proportions from nature. The trunks of trees serve as columns, while the branching crown provides inspiration for the creation of the ornate Corinthian capital. This is the explanation given by M. Ribart de Chamoust in his work *L'Ordre François Trouvé dans la Nature* (1783).

appeared. What remains of his ideas are sprawling and unattractive residential areas in the suburbs of cities.

It is true that several decades later the idea of garden cities contributed to another attempt to achieve a balance between the rural hinterland and the inhospitable town made of brick and stone. Satellite towns were invented.

Houses with gardens are not a typical feature of satellite towns. Housing is more like that of a traditional town, including streets, squares and multi-storey buildings. However, with regard to their size and population, satellite towns are smaller settlements situated close to large cities with which they are economically, socially and culturally linked by means of transport systems.

The name 'satellite town' was probably used for the first time in 1919 as a substitute for Welwyn, even though Leonar-

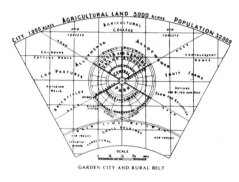

A diagram for a garden city published by Ebenezer Howard in 1898. It was an attempt to find the most favourable combination of built-up area, the number of inhabitants who were to live in this area, and the agricultural hinterland separating similar settlements from one another. Howard emphasizes that he is merely offering an idealized vision which has to be adapted to the possibilities provided by nature or the landscape.

A Welwyn Garden City advertisement from 1919, which summarizes the main principles of the Garden City Movement: it draws attention to the bleak living conditions endured in industrialized regions and casts doubt on half-hearted improvements which bring no real solutions. The proposed design of such a garden city is seen as the only way forward.

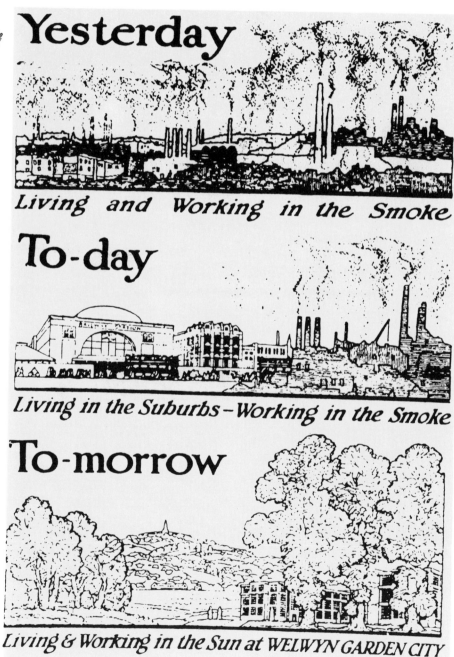

113

do da Vinci had suggested a similar arrangement of settlement at the end of the 15th century. He proposed to decrease the population of plague-threatened Milan in this manner.

The construction of satellite towns was intended by some architects and sociologists to lessen the burden on large cities which were becoming unmanageable and unfit for ordinary habitation. Satellite towns are an improvement because of their size and access to the countryside even though their inhabitants want to retain close links with nearby metropolises. The Greater London project by Leslie Patrick Abercrombie, an English architect, is a typical example. It inspired the foundation of several new satellite towns between thirty and fifty kilometres from London (the original project planned settlements of some 50,000—70,000 inhabitants). Some of them, for example Harlow, Stevenage and Hemel Hempstead, represent remarkable attempts at a new type of settlement.

Other ideas on urban construction have not been realized but in many aspects they have influenced the contemporary town. For example, in 1920 the German architect Bruno Taut forecast the dispersal of towns to an idealized countryside. Le Corbusier's projects of a 'Radiant City' (Ville Radieuse) submitted several years later are a special type of a garden city consisting of high-rise buildings built among urban parks.

They are in contrast to Howard's small garden cities with low-rise family houses. The American architect Frank Lloyd Wright designed a project rejecting the town's structure as it has evolved. His hygienic, airy 'Broadacre City' allocates at least one acre of land to each inhabitant.

Only one hundred years ago people believed that the crowded and neglected towns would improve if the old-fashioned town walls disappeared. They pulled them down, but this was simply not enough. It seemed that it might help if

Spreading suburbia. The result of attempts to escape from the confines of the city and to get closer to Nature.

towns were dotted with green town gardens and parks. But it was like eating the crumbs of a stale cake hoping that it might become tastier.

However, available sites where modern settlement could be built have been exhausted if we are not to waste valuable agricultural land and destroy the countryside completely. The less enclosed, dispersed layout of some modern cities where the density of settlement is achieved by the height of buildings and the number of flats on each floor is not a happy solution as our everyday experience tells us.

It does not put us closer in touch with Nature. Asphalt and concrete roads, huge parking lots and withered grass force out fresh and healthy living. We are left with an acute sense of disappointment at our failure to construct the town of our dreams whose life would be inseparably intertwined and interlinked with the surrounding countryside.

The Hanging Gardens of Babylon Copied in Modern Cities

There is another means of moving closer to Nature. The city cannot be scattered throughout the countryside but we can take nature, the countryside with its trees and bushes, into the city. These can become part of the city's integral structure.

One example is a roof garden. Nature has been incorporated in towns in this manner for at least two mil-

The Hanging Gardens of Queen Semiramis as they might have looked.

lennia, according to archaeological excavations. The earliest finds are from the Near East, from the period of the rule of King Solomon (the 10th century B.C.).

The Hanging Gardens of Babylon established during the reign of King Nebuchadnezzar were one of the Seven Wonders of the Ancient World. At that time the two fundamental problems of roof gardens, which still cause headaches for modern builders, were successfully resolved: proper insulation which would prevent dampness from affecting the building itself, and providing a sufficient amount of moisture for the shrubs and bushes.

Murals and frescoes from ancient Rome confirm that roof gardens were common in most palaces and patricians' houses. People grew plants in huge containers on terraces, which was neither complicated nor expensive. The tomb of Augustus (Emperor 27 B.C. — A.D. 14) was an outstanding example. The structure which had a diameter of ninety metres was decorated with a terrace complete with cyprus trees and plants in movable containers.

As mentioned previously, the Renaissance period drew inspiration from classical models. Roof gardens were common in Italian Renaissance towns. For example,

around A.D. 1400 the Medici Palace in Florence was built with terraces and a roof garden covering an area over 1,000 square metres.

These structures were usually complex and expensive. The invention of reinforced concrete in 1867, which has since enabled a more advanced construction of roofs and entire buildings, was a major step forward. The advantages of this new construction material became evident in 1887 when it was used for the first roof garden on top of a residential house in Lombardy.

New technological procedures and more resilient construction materials seemed to

115

Left, below, right:
In addition to countries and towns, 17th century maps by Dutch cartographers also depicted gardens. The town is considered to be a safer and more comfortable environment, sheltered from the more chaotic world beyond the town walls. Bushes and trees cultivated in a human settlement had not yet come to be seen as an expression of the need to return to Nature. They were carefully planted, and shaped to form green areas, which were pleasurable in so far as they offered a more interesting perspective or some welcome shade. They became isolated from Nature by man.

A street poster invites us to the urban environment of a garden restaurant. Parks have been cultivated in towns since the second half of the 19th century. Urban planners allocated space for greenery in those areas where the most extensive conurbations occurred, particularly where buildings were demolished and reconstructed, as in Paris or Vienna. Urban gardens and parks have been laid out on vacated building land, in place of demolished town walls or where vineyards or suburban orchards used to be.

▼

▲

Homes originating from living, growing trees. Artur Wiechula began to promote these in his book, first published in 1925. He uses trees and bushes as building material. In some aspects he copies Renaissance and Baroque gardeners. But as he lives in the 20th century, he gives economic reasons for his theory of utilizing trees by proposing savings on bricks and wood, as well as on roofing material. His strange, forgotten work has been revived in recent discussions on ecologically sound construction.

provide hope that roof gardens, until this time unusual features, might became common in towns. However, this has not been the case.

Those who advocate ecological housing quote Le Corbusier that roof gardens should have a major role to play in the city as a whole and in one's own home. Nevertheless, the final result seems to contradict this. Increasingly, there are more flat roofs but instead of flower beds and shrubs they have merely been insulated or covered with metal sheets or asphalt coating. The green dream disappears in the grey uniformity of flat roofs.

The ecological movement has developed since the 1970s. Its advocates have attempted to revive the dream of the Hanging Gardens of Babylon. The developments of the chemical industry, and particularly the invention of insulation materials, have contributed to the success of similar experiments. We now know which pollution resistant plants are suitable for growing in towns. Nature can become more than a decorative element. There are attempts to use some kinds of plants as a construction material — so that, in fact, some houses grow out of tree roots. Plants may even replace roof coverings or the insulation casing of houses.

Self-Sufficiency and the City

The inhabitants of the earliest cities were supplied with wheat and barley by nearby farmers. The town dwellers could regulate and influence the supply of foodstuffs directly. In addition, transport from more distant areas would have been uneconomical.

The inhabitants of the first Greek cities were also aware of their dependence on the fertility of the surrounding area. It provided them with nourishment and also construction materials. They carefully considered how large their settlement might be in order that it would not disturb the natural balance between man and the surrounding farmed countryside.

We can observe even in paintings of medieval towns that domestic animals, such as goats, pigs or hens, were a feature of urban life. The town and the countryside were separated by town walls but the sources of nourishment were close at hand.

The balance between the city and its rural hinterland changed significantly during the Industrial Revolution. Britain was the first country which began to exchange its manufactured goods for cheaper foodstuffs and raw materials imported from distant colonies. Its example was soon followed by most other European countries. The links between towns and their rural hinterlands began to break down. It became possible to feed more people than the fields and farms immediately beyond town walls could. This was, at first, the most important consideration.

However, this pseudo-ad-

Each era focuses on the debate of topical issues. The fuel crisis of the 1970s drew attention to energy issues. The relationship between nature and a residential house is shown by a diagram whose principles have been employed, at least partially, in the construction of many houses. The green carpet on the roof insulates in addition to improving the environment. In summer, as visible from the upper drawing, the trees in front of the house provide shade, and they function as a natural air-conditioning system, together with the flowers and bushes growing in the hothouse attached to the southern façade. In winter, when the leaves fall, the sun, which is low on the horizon, heats residential rooms via the hothouse.

An idealized view of a closed-cycle ecological economy in a growing city.

link between the city and the countryside flourished, most refuse was re-used, for example as manure.

It should be realized that the inhabitants of New York produce so much refuse, sewage and kitchen left-overs annually that these would cover the entire 340 hectares of New York's Central Park to a height of four metres. The bigger the city is, the less easy is it to recycle at least part of its refuse and return it to Nature as a nutrient.

Nevertheless, many cities have been attempting to do this. In the Bronx, one of the less salubrious parts of New York, accumulated heaps of refuse have actually helped to improve several streets. This unusual example demonstrates that much can be done if people are serious in their attempts to re-create their link with Nature. In the southern part of the Bronx an empty area of 750 acres was left after housing demolition. How could this space be utilised? Somebody came up with the idea of turning the rubble and piles of rubbish into garden allotments. The advocates of this idea soon discovered that there was a vegetable market nearby. It produced 50 to 70 tonnes of organic waste daily. Using new compost making technology, common on large farms, the burdensome vegetable material was turned into first-rate compost after several weeks of turning, mixing and maturing. In the same growing season, plants on several flower beds blossomed; next to them toma-

vantage soon brought about new problems. It started a vicious cycle of town growth, since the more people a town could feed the more arrived expecting to be fed. Increasing industrial production provided more job opportunities. It was no longer necessary to value the countryside beyond the town walls as the town became dependent on different resources and influences. Much of the former agricultu-

ral land changed into devastated or build-up areas.

Where does this imbalance lead to? Life in a city becomes more expensive and unhealthy. The consumption of energy increases — more energy is consumed for transport, for food preparation and heating homes. Energy is also consumed disposing of waste and rubbish, which become a problem and nuisance for the city. In the past when the

119

toes, water melons and maize ripened. This was a novel experience for many local children; there was no other place in the city where they could have observed vegetables growing and maturing.

Vegetation makes a somewhat unconventional return to places from which it has been forced out by many generations of city dwellers. Vegetable production and ornate gardens which use humus formed from decomposed organic waste are quite common in most towns. Hong Kong is a special example. It has over five million inhabitants living on a small area of only one thousand square kilometres. However, the town gardens provide the city with over half its fresh vegetables. Kitchen scraps from houses and restaurants feed pigs which account for most of the pork consumed in Hong Kong.

Trees and bushes lining the streets and urban squares are like houseplants. They indicate that somebody lives in the place, that it is not abandoned. But we have to care for houseplants or else they will wither and die. Small green islands planted repeatedly in the town can help to overcome uniformity and the depressing greyness of its streets. And they can also help the city itself to survive.

In Addition

It is increasingly difficult to preserve traces of Nature in an environment swamped by cars and exposed to industrial pollution, in the midst of ever growing deserts of stone, cement and asphalt communications. Evidently, fresh and healthy plants improve a town's climate. The buildings and road surfaces absorb and store heat resulting in the so-called 'furnace-effect' or a 'thermal cloud' above the city, which raises the local temperature above that of the surrounding countryside. Hot air currents above the city centre suck colder air from the surrounding areas and lift dust particles, impurities and other pollutants. These create a form of dust curtain above the city. Conversely, trees, bushes, shrubs and green grass create moisture and cool the air, also enriching it with oxygen. They absorb dirt and pollution. We can plant various species of trees, clumps of shrubs, climbing plants and flower beds in places where previously we missed them or even where we never expected them to appear. Planting can create front gardens outside residential blocks of flats and can enliven courtyards previously used only by parked cars. Trees and shrubs can line the streets, separate public spaces from private ones and they can unify disparate architectural styles. Climbing plants can decorate the façades of houses, box hedges can lessen traffic noise. It is obvious that this requires time and patience, not to mention the cost, but such an approach brings clear rewards. After all, one mature tree can do as much to improve the urban climate as one hectare of grass.

A Guide to the Historical Labyrinth

1920 — The establishment of another garden city, Welwyn Garden City in England.

1920 — Bruno Taut (1880—1938), a German architect and urban planner, published his book Die Auflösung der Städte (The Dispersal of the Towns); its title became the slogan for the anti-urbanization movement (rejecting the concentration of people in towns) which appeared in the first half of the 20th century.

1920 — Greater Prague was established by the inclusion of 37 formerly independent villages and towns within the city boundaries. This marked the modern development of the capital city of an independent Czechoslovakia.

1922 — Le Corbusier (Charles Edouard Jeanneret), the French architect and urban planner who has significantly influenced modern town planning, exhibited at the Paris Autumn Salon his project for a Contemporary City (Ville Contemporaine) of three million inhabitants.

1923 — An earthquake with its epicentre on the Pacific Coast killed 70,000 inhabitants of Tokyo — 300,000 houses were destroyed — 30,000 inhabitants of Yokohama and 14,000 inhabitants in other regions.

1924 — Le Corbusier's Urbanisme was published. It was supplemented with his plan for the reconstruction of Paris (Plan Voisin de Paris).

1928 — The CIAM (Congrès Internationaux d'Architecture Moderne), the most important international association linking the proponents of modern architecture and urbanism, was established. In 1933 the participants at the fourth CIAM Congress, devoted to the issues of a functional town, adopted the fundamental principles for planning a modern city. This became known as the Athenian Charter.

1928 — The construction of Radburn, an unconventional garden city near New York. It was interrupted a year later because of the Depression. This first garden town was designed by C. Stein; his ideas were influential in the Greenbelt City Movement of the 1930s.

1943 — Leslie Patrick Abercrombie (1879—1957), a British urban planner's project for Greater London; this proposed the construction of satellite towns around the Metropolis. This Greater London Project was approved by the Houses of Parliament in 1946; the New Town Act dealing with the construction of new towns was also adopted in the same year.

1949—54 — A project was proposed and the construction began of Chandigarh, a new administrative capital for East Punjab in India; Le Corbusier acted as advisor to the project and designed its Capitol.

1952 — The construction of Tapiola on the outskirts of Helsinki, the capital of Finland. This garden satellite town merges harmoniously a modern human settlement with its environment.

1960 — The newly built Brasilia, designed by the architects Lúcio Costa and Oscar Niemeyer, became the capital of Brazil.

1960 — New York's Museum of Modern Art held an exhibition of Visionary Architecture; it included fanciful projects for towns.

1963 — C. A. Doxiadis, a Greek architect and urban planner, established the Athenian Centre of Ecostics, i.e. the study of human settlements.

1965 — New York experienced a twelve hour breakdown in supplies of electricity, water and natural gas; in this era of technology it was the first real test of the sensitive workings of a modern city; a similar 25 hour breakdown occurred in 1977 with, however, more serious consequences.

1965 — A territorial plan for Paris based its further development on newly founded towns, situated about thirty kilometres from the city. By the 1990s most of these towns had been built.

1973 — The construction of the Sears Tower in Chicago, which is currently the world's tallest skyscraper.

1976 — A U.N. Conference on Human Settlements took place in Vancouver, Canada. It represented a major step forward in current theories on contemporary towns as ecological aspects became most fundamental; the United Nations Centre for Human Settlements — Habitat — was established.

VII *A Gateway to the Future*

Future expectations are undoubtedly influenced by one's personal experience. People in each historical era have their own ideas which often have less to do with an imagined future than what has burdened them in the past. Seen from this perspective we can leaf through a multitude of architectural projects and treatises concerning the future development of urban settlement. Some of them are great works of literature, whereas others are mere technical descriptions.

Utopia

At the time when the sailing ships of European seafarers were first criss-crossing the world's oceans, look-outs were anxiously searching for 'land on the horizon'. True stories which sounded fantastic were told throughout Europe of far-off lands, strange towns and exotic plants and herbs. In 1516 Hernán Cortés landed on the shores of Mexico. That same year Marten's printing works at Louvain in Flanders produced the first copies of a unique book. Some people might have believed that it was just another eyewitness account describing one of the many newly discovered lands, just another of those ship's logs or travel narratives. This tale of a strange island with a most justly administered human community was, however, fictional.

It was written in Latin by Sir Thomas More (1478—1535) and translated into English under the title *A Fruiteful and pleasunt worke of the beste State of a public weale, and of the new yle, called Utopia*. It is written in the form of an imaginary dialogue between More and a traveller, one Rafael Hythloday in Antwerp. He has discovered the island of 'Utopia', 'Nowhere land', and since his return from those vast, unmapped seas, he has entertained all with his tales.

Contemporary enthusiasm for overseas discoveries and the yearning for adventure served as a framework for these remarkable speculations of Sir Thomas More, an important English statesman, humanist and Renaissance man. His traveller did not discover riches, as was common in the fanciful travellers' tales of that time, but provided future generations with numerous ideas on how to organize human society in the best way to create the ideal environment for man.

The inhabitants of the imaginary island of Utopia observed strict but just laws. Everybody had enough to eat and somewhere to live in appropriate comfort. There were no poor nor rich there but this was achieved, as Rafael, the traveller, says, with the condition that 'no man sit idle but that every one apply his own craft with earnest diligence'. People scorned luxury and riches and every free minute was bestowed upon some science which was ultimately to lead to an understanding of the world's laws and man's place in that world. The main activity was husbandry, which was the fundamental source of nourishment. Every two years the inhabitants of fifty-four cities of Utopia exchanged places with the country folk. In the cities people devoted themselves to crafts and to the building or repairing of houses. This exchange was an attempt to remove the differences between the countryside and the town which resulted from different work occupations and which was also reflected in their dwellings. The exchange might also have been intended as a protection against the evils of urban life such as self-indulgence and profligacy, various vices and criminality, which are common to any great conglomeration of people. More, himself, was familiar with these pitfalls from the London streets of the early 16th century.

The Utopian cities created an interlinked network of settlements situated at a distance of approximately one day's walk from each other. The most dignified city of Amaurote in the middle of the island served as 'the chief and head city'. More used it to articulate his general principles on urban life in the ideal society.

Amaurote was situated on the banks of the River Anyder, 'in fashion almost foursquare'. Rafael provides a detailed description: 'The city is compassed about with a high and thick stone wall full of turrets and bulwarks. A dry ditch, but deep and broad and overgrown with bushes, briars, and thorns, goeth about three sides or quarters of the city. To the fourth side the river itself serveth for a ditch. The streets be appointed and set forth very commodious and handsome, both for carriage and also against the winds. The houses be of fair and gorgeous building, and on the street side they stand joined together in a long row through the whole street without any partition or separation.'

More tells us that Amaurote had a gravity water supply, which was uncommon in European towns at this time. Amaurote had large and well equipped hospitals in the 'circuit of the city', and its gardens were nicely kept. Every ward had a large hall to which citizens were invited 'by the noise of a brazen trumpet at the set hours of dinner and supper'. There were 'neither wine taverns, nor alehouses, nor stews, nor any occasion of vice or wickedness . . .'. The shape of the cities held strictly to a unified and commonly beneficial order. In the words of Rafael, 'whoso knoweth one of them knoweth them all, they be all so like one to another as far forth as the nature of the place permitteth.'

It is remarkable that More's *Utopia* has ultimately become more famous than many real islands on whose shores explorers and conquistadores, devout missionaries and reckless adventurers landed. The Utopia created by More's imagination (the name comes from the Greek 'u' = no, and 'topos' = place, i.e. a 'Nowhere land' which does not exist) has inspired and given the name to extensive Utopian literature

Cities on the imaginary island of Utopia. An introductory illustration from 1516 for the first edition of Thomas More's *Utopia*.

and projects for Utopian towns. Such reforms and projects are impractical, attempting to realize something that is not possible under existing conditions. The unusual name — Hythloday — speaks volumes about the reliability of the narrator himself: it, too, comes from Greek, 'hythlos' = bosh, balderdash, and 'daios' = experienced. It is also a pointer to the sources of More's *Utopia* which seem to have been taken from works of ancient philosophers, especially Plato's *Republic* and *Laws*.

In fact, Plato (427—347 B.C.) was the progenitor of urban Utopias, particularly as he attempted to overcome existing problems through the strict organization of urban environments and civic life; the individual's private interest were subordinated to the public interest.

Plato's doctrines, and More's ideas also, influenced Tommaso Campanella, an Italian Dominican friar (1568 to 1639), who wrote his *Città del Sole* in prison. The City of the Sun was a community of people living in a fortified city. The city was circular in shape and subdivided into seven fortified zones. The inhabitants passed from one zone to another through gates. Along four paved roads they reached the centre where a circular temple stood on a mound. Positioned against the inner fortified walls were residential palaces used by all the city dwellers, i.e. a kind of communal living which is

ever popular in Utopian literature and science fiction. In the first half of the twentieth century several communal buildings, such as the French Unité, were built but they were not judged a success. Living in them was not pleasant.

Campanella's communal palaces combined in a continuous line alongside the fortifications and their walls were decorated with splendid murals depicting all the sciences in an unusually perfect arrangement. They were an extensive pictorial encyclopaedia, from stars and mathematical formulae, maps of lands and countries, to minerals, plants, fish, birds, snakes and insects accompanied by commentaries on these animals' habitats, their lives and usefulness to man. The walls also showed pictures of crafts, tools and methods used in work. In addition, portraits of inventors and scientists, politicians and military heroes were included. When a man went out for a walk he was simultaneously learning and improving his mind. Between the ages of two and three, children out for a walk, who pass the walls of the palaces, learn to speak and to recognize the alphabet; at the age of eight they learn the basics of mathematics from the murals; later they learn the natural sciences. Campanella reminded us of the importance of a town's environment for establishing people's attitudes. He indicated some of the possibilities for influencing people's thinking and behaviour.

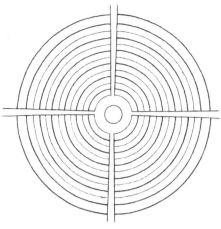

Tommaso Campanella's *Città del Sole* of 1602. Seven circles of fortified walls delineated the direction of the streets; in the centre stood a circular temple on a mound.

The Search for a New Atlantis

Francis Bacon (1561—1626), an English philosopher and statesman, was Campanella's contemporary. Bacon's contribution to Utopian theories was rather unusual. In the *New Atlantis*, he describes 'Solomon's House' on a distant island in the Pacific, which is a special college dedicated to the development of science and technology and the gathering of existing knowledge and information. Science has for its end, as the narrator tells Bacon, 'enlarging of the Bounds of Human Empire, to the effecting of all things possible.' Thus, a 17th century reader was astounded by incredible technical discoveries, machines and fantastic apparatus. Solomon's House was an inspiration for the writers of Utopian literature and the authors of Utopian projects. It forecast one of the most striking features

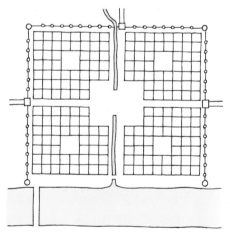

The composition of the ideal human habitat Amaurote, the capital of Utopia. It was almost square, divided into four quarters, each with a central market and each providing a home to about 1,500 families. Each quarter was subdivided into smaller blocks, or wards, with a large hall which served as a meeting place for 30 families.

of the future society — incredible scientific and technical advances. In addition to being astonished by the descriptions of machinery and inventions, 17th century readers became more confident about man's abilities. These new possibilities suddenly seemed more attractive than romantic pictures of imaginary lands.

As more new towns appeared in the world, new cities created through the imagination of writers also appeared. Their works had a moral and educational purpose. One of them is Jan Amos Komenský's (Comenius's) *Orbis sensualium pictus* from 1623 (published in English in 1659 as Comenius's Visible World), depicting the entire world as a single, extended and fortified city.

In 1771, Louis Sébastien Mercier travelled in a dream to the year 2440. He did not require 'the time machine' of modern science fiction in order to be able to inspect the cities of the first half of the 3rd millennium. He writes that he found himself on pleasant, wide and regularly built streets. He stressed that the crossroads were spacious, so that there was order, without any confusion or chaos. He could not hear any unpleasant noise which had previously assaulted his ears. In addition, as if in contrast to his own experience, Mercier did not encounter any carriages which tried to run him over, and everyone who wished to could walk comfortably. Another Utopian work, Morelly's *Code de la nature*, from the second half of the 18th century, summarizes concisely but prosaically the rules for founding a future society, without any colourful literary imagery. These laws restrict the uncontrollable growth of settlements. They allow for the functional division of the city, into residential areas, a civic centre, a row of craft workshops and finally farm barns and cowsheds in the outskirts. The city has a home for the elderly and a hospital built upon the healthiest site outside the city. The cleanliness of town communities and public roads is regularly maintained by the guilds of roadmen and carters.

Dreams Beyond the Horizons of the Industrial Revolution

Literary imagination no longer sufficed as practical considerations became more important. Nevertheless, the term 'Utopia' was retained for treatises and schemes which replaced the narratives of the 16th century sailors and travellers. These authors took their ideas seriously, elaborated upon them with dogged perseverance and struggled to put them into practice. In a way, they reflected life in late 18th and early 19th century towns, with their print works, engineering works, mines, steel mills and cotton mills, which were surrounded by endless workers' houses, dirty and cramped, which allowed for mere survival. Unfortunately, these ideas and schemes were too advanced and idealised for their time, society and the world.

Robert Owen (1771—1858), an English socialist and philanthropist, noted that the industrial cities were the seats of poverty, vice, crime and deprivation. He rejected large cities and proposed the establishment of model workers' communities. They were to consist of an enclosed complex of buildings around a large square. At most, two to two and a half thousand people were to live in these communities. Some of them were to look after the fields and animals while others were to work in manufacturing. In Owen's description such a model community combined the pleasures of town and country residence, excluding all their disadvantages, and was surrounded by parkland measuring 2,000—3,000 acres.

Owen was not just a dreamer. He was a successful, wealthy businessman who proceeded to set up his model community of New Lanark in Scotland. Later, he established another community overseas in America. New Harmony was founded in 1825. There Owen attempted to introduce—without major success—his principles of payment according to need, a non-pecuniary economy and a collective life. He also promoted infant schools and other educational establishments. Nowadays, 150 years later, New Harmony, a small town on the River Wabash in Indiana, is still visited by tour-

Gustave Doré: A 19th-century town.

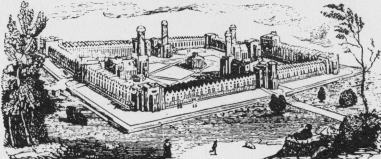

THE CRISIS,

OR THE CHANGE FROM ERROR AND MISERY, TO TRUTH AND HAPPINESS

1832.

IF WE CANNOT YET   RECONCILE ALL OPINIONS,

LET US ENDEAVOUR   TO UNITE ALL HEARTS.

IT IS OF ALL TRUTHS THE MOST IMPORTANT, THAT THE CHARACTER OF MAN IS FORMED FOR — NOT BY HIMSELF.

Design of a Community of 2,000 Persons, founded upon a principle, commended by Plato, Lord Bacon, Sir T. More, & R. Owen.

EDITED BY

ROBERT OWEN AND ROBERT DALE OWEN.

London:

PRINTED AND PUBLISHED BY J. EAMONSON, 15, CHICHESTER PLACE
GRAY'S INN ROAD.

STRANGE. PATERNOSTER ROW. PURKISS, OLD COMPTON STREET.
AND MAY BE HAD OF ALL BOOKSELLERS.

Robert Owen's book *The Crisis*. Its cover depicts an architectonic plan of an ideal settlement for 2,000 inhabitants. The author stresses that the community should be based on the principles formulated by Plato, Bacon, Sir Thomas More, and ... Robert Owen.

ists and experts in the field of town planning. Like New Lanark in Scotland, it reminds us of a utopian, failed experiment which, nevertheless, was a remarkable attempt to create a human environment which would improve living conditions and shape man's character.

Charles Fourier (1772 — 1837), a French utopian socialist, also suggested the establishment of industrial towns. His words sound a cautious note: 'The air like the land is misused by industrial production. Our descendants will one day curse our civilization ...'.

Fourier intended to prevent the concentration of industry by dispersed settlements, composed of ideal communities or 'phalanxes'. Each phalanx was a voluntary grouping of 400—500 families which functioned as a self-sufficient cooperative. They produced foodstuffs by farming on allo-

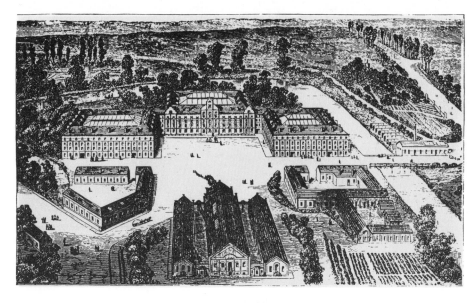

A concept illustration of Fourier's 'Familistère' by V. Considérant.

'From the 20th Century Wonders...'. A futuristic appearance of a European settlement in illustrations accompanying an imaginary vision by A. Robida from the end of the 19th century. He was enchanted by the popular technological inventions of his days.

cated land while they made other goods in factories. The population of each phalanx lived in a 'phalanstery', a spacious building of unusual architectural design. They used a common dining hall, club rooms and games halls; all year round they could go for a walk in a covered air-conditioned gallery. Fourier designed technical equipment for them, including economical central heating, a wireless telegraph and speedy transport. The aim was to achieve 'a system of world harmony', by co-ordinating individual interests and happiness with the needs and scope of the entire community through the proper organization of work in phalanxes and by directing human emotions.

In 1859, some enthusiasts attempted to realize Fourier's ideals under the name 'Familistère' in France. However, most of these 'phalanxes' col-

At the end of the 19th century, Edward Bellamy, a Utopian novelist, together with many important architects of the day, participated in a discussion on how a future city might look. This is Bellamy's view of a London street in the year 2000.

133

lapsed within five years of their foundation. Human life is too complex to be planned in all its minute details in advance and then constrained within Utopian schemes.

Further Horizons

This era has been full of technological and scientific discoveries which changed the world and promoted the hectic development of industrial production. This brought about a boundless confidence in new inventions which reached the streets and ordinary homes in the form of beneficial devices. In the 1810s, London's streets were lit for the first time by gas lighting, thus removing at a stroke the previously unbridgeable gap between night and day. In America Oliver Evans's amphibious steam powered vehicle made a journey of a few miles by land and water. It looked like a replica of vehicles illustrated in science fiction. Long before

the invention of the first automobile, inventors had been searching for a faster and more convenient form of transport. In 1809, Robert Stevens made the first sea voyage in a paddle wheel steamer, smaller replicas of which later appeared on many rivers which flowed through cities. In the 1820s, George Stevenson's steam locomotive the *Rocket* travelling at 30 miles an hour opened up the possibility of faster trains in the future. Builders were installing central heating with ribbed radiators in residential houses. There had been attempts to use electricity for lighting purposes long before Thomas Alva Edison was even born.

It was so tempting to let the imagination run wild—encouraged, for example, by the strange chemical process of the first photographs or the 1840 Pittsburgh Suspension Bridge hanging on spidery steel cables. In addition, early experiments with the telephone to transmit a human voice (and, in time, perhaps even a human face) over long distances together with the possibilities of further forms of mass communications later resulted in the schemes and visions for the dispersed settlement . . . .

The existing mood provided inspiration and encouragement for the authors of Utopias. Centuries earlier, More and Campanella were also influenced in a similar manner — their ideal cities were derived from many actual Renaissance towns but, in addition, they attempted to reorganize the personal lives of the inhabitants and their relationships.

The architecture of Utopian cities seems to outstrip their own era but very often it was actually based on existing human knowledge with a liberal addition of imagination. Imagination helps to overcome

those obstacles which in themselves cannot be solved by scientific discoveries and technological inventions. Mankind places much faith in science and technology. We can observe the same attitude in modern visions which attempt to resolve the vast sprawl of towns, or 'town explosion', which is one of the most acute problems of our times.

The Huge Spread of Cities

The United Nations demographers warn that we are witnessing the biggest population shift in human history. At the beginning of the 20th century, London was the only city which had five million inhabitants. By the early 1980s there were twenty-six five million or five million plus cities in the world. It is likely that by the year 2000 there will be sixty cities with over five million inhabitants. Of these, forty seven will be situated in developing countries and have a low standard of technical and social infrastructures. At present one in four inhabitants of city conglomerations in the developing world already lives in a slum, a favella or a barrio — underground or in primitive sheds built of mud or corrugated iron. In the 1920s only fourteen per cent of the world's population lived in towns. Fifty years later it was already forty per cent, approximately 1.8 billion people. In North America three quarters of the population live in towns, in Europe about seventy per cent. These

Cities are places where great numbers of people congregate, and also places where social problems tend to be concentrated. These, in turn, give rise to catastrophic visions of future urban habitats, where the solution offered is their ultimate destruction. This is depicted in the illustrations for *The End of the World* by the French astronomer Camille Flammarion, which was published in the 1890s.

are the most urbanized regions of the world and, therefore, the movement to towns is slower at present. The principal remaining problem is, however, the high concentration of town populations and the spreading of urban settlements and conurbations.

There have also been 'town explosions' in African and Asian countries, in addition to some Latin American cities.

The town populations have increased primarily because of the growing numbers of people living in the world. There are approximately 5.5 billion people in the world. It is estimated that the world will have more than 6 billion people by the end of the 20th century. According to the estimate of the United Nations,

World's Ten Largest Metropolitan Areas, by millions of people in 1950, 1980, and 2000

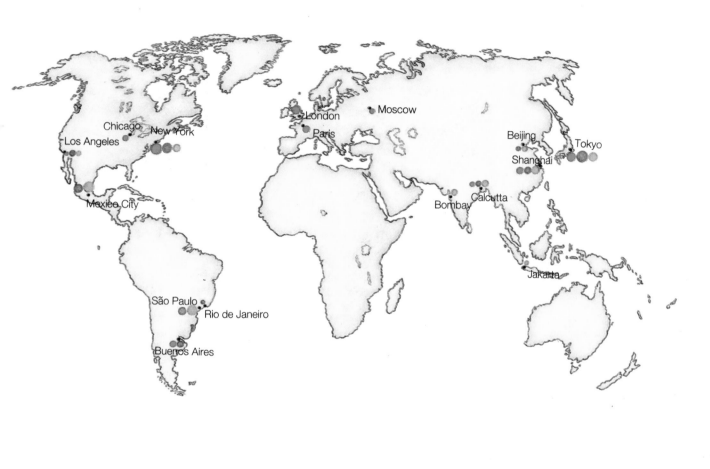

● 1950		● 1980		● 2000 (projections)	
1. New York	12.3	Tokyo	16.9	Mexico City	25.6
2. London	8.7	New York	15.6	São Paulo	22.1
3. Tokyo	6.7	Mexico City	14.5	Tokyo	19.0
4. Paris	5.4	São Paulo	12.1	Shanghai	17.0
5. Shanghai	5.3	Shanghai	11.7	New York	16.8
6. Buenos Aires	5.0	Buenos Aires	9.9	Calcutta	15.7
7. Chicago	4.9	Los Angeles	9.5	Bombay	15.4
8. Moscow	4.8	Calcutta	9.0	Beijing	14.0
9. Calcutta	4.4	Beijing	9.0	Los Angeles	13.9
10. Los Angeles	4.0	Rio de Janeiro	8.8	Jakarta	13.7

The ten largest conurbations in the world (according to the statistics and estimate of the United Nations): a comparison of their development until 1950, their position in 1980 and expected changes by the year 2000. The colour coding shows which regions of the world have experienced the greatest increase in numbers of the largest 'metropolitan areas'.

towns and cities will be a home for more than a half of the world's population. This is a very important consideration when we look beyond the horizon of the contemporary city.

New Utopias

The merciless urbanization of our planet becomes the main focus for Utopian and visionary projects. We can often recognize in them modern towers of Babel, super-skyscrapers and tower cities. The drawings of W. Chalk, P. Morgan, P. Maymont or M. M. Cotti take the form of complex suspended constructions or pylons with adequate numbers of exchangeable housing units. Other visions are funnel-shaped, pointing heavenwards in order that they might occupy the smallest possible areas of essential land.

The fears that there might be a lack of space for the world's increasing population led to the design of huge constructions situated on platforms above the sea's surface, already built-up sites or fields. Yona Friedman, a French architect, designed an extensive city conglomeration to be situated above Paris. Kenzo Tange, a Japanese architect, submitted his design for a modern Venice situated above an inlet of the sea near overpopulated Tokyo.

Another visionary residential structure named the 'Plug-in-City' by Archigram, a group of British architects, also aroused a great deail of interest. It consists of a huge spa-

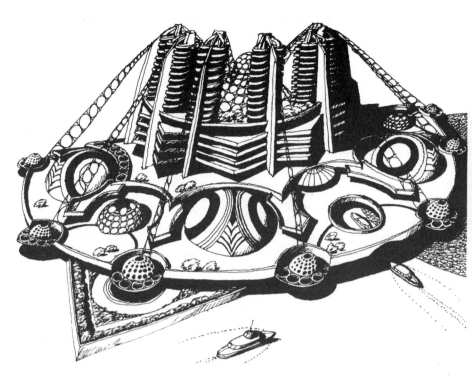

Architectonic utopias of the latter half of the 20th century comprise, firstly, those which search for a new approach to vast residential megastructures, influenced, in many respects, by the experience gained when building the 20th century cities: (a) — F. Lloyd Wright's design of a residential structure on Ellis Island in New York Bay, which resembles the structures on nearby Manhattan Island. Secondly, they embrace designs which rely on a technological solution offered by the latest construction technologies (b) — for example, a Japanese Aquapolis by the architect K. Kikutake. And, lastly, are late 20th century Utopias for which inspiration from historical towns seems to be an unrealizable fantasy when compared with the development of settlements in the 20th century (c) — e.g. Atlantis by Leon Krier.

cial construction in which, according to need, depreciation and changing fashion, individual residential cells or even larger parts of the city may be replaced or new ones gradually added. The same group of architects also suggested a city which could 'walk' and move to a more suitable site. It would behave in the same manner as nomads have done for centuries.

The vast oceans and their potential seem to pose an eternal challenge. Their extensive surfaces could become inexhaustible sites for floating cities. One of the best known visions is that of the 'Tetrahentonal City' by Buckminster Fuller, an American architect.

He submitted this highly elaborate plan for a floating satellite island on Lake Ontario of Toronto, Canada. It was intended to provide a home for about three million people, or 300,000 families, each of which would have a flat covering 200 square metres, plus a spacious terrace and a garden.

Buckminster Fuller has also designed a complex of similar oceanic city islands. He suggested the use of construction materials from demolished buildings on the mainland. He did not envisage the construction of cities for millions of inhabitants from the very beginning but the building of smaller settlements for about one thousand people which would be enlarged gradually and completed according to an ingenious system. In this manner, the settlement in unused regions of the world's oceans would gradually proceed. This process would be somewhat similar to medieval town colonization.

Gerard O'Neill, a Professor of Physics, however, stresses that even now the world as such is too small. He suggests searching for more living accommodation in space. He says that he began to consider projects in space cities by chance in 1969 when he spoke with his Princeton University students about the worsening living conditions on our planet. O'Neill's space city only resembles spacecraft technology from the outside. The living quarters would be enclosed within a residential cylinder, a ring or a sphere, which would create artificial gravity

rotating along the axis. O'Neill situated a system of mirrors above his space city, which would create the illusion of a moving sky and Sun. He proposed only a part of the available concave area for the city itself, planned for about 9 million inhabitants, as he also allocated a certain area to agricultural production, in addition to an area for recreation in an artificially created 'return to nature'. O'Neill, who as a scientist and an expert, was well aware of the possibilities and limitations of space technology, also provided solutions for numerous detailed problems. His long-term experience also led him to the conclusion that it might be necessary to regulate human emotions in this unusual, enclosed and unnatural environment, and to adapt imperfect people to their perfect artificial surroundings.

Back to the Earth

Is an escape to space the only or the best way in which man can change and transform his environment?

In addition to the gigantic scale and grandeur of these cities, their authors' unbounded confidence in overcoming any potential obstacles makes these projects most attractive. Their proponents make them seem more viable by being certain that their solution is by far the best and the only solution. They are not concerned with trifling complications, such as individual needs and feelings. They seem to disregard the

New projects in the cities at the end of the 20th century furnish streets and squares with benches, kerbs, eye-catching poster art, colourful canopies above shops, vending machines, telephone boxes, bus shelters, in addition to street lamps and waste bins whose shape and size correspond to the contemporary lifestyle. A pedestrian uses and perceives the city through these objects, whether they are important or trivial. They are a reminder that time does not stand still in the streets.

140

fact that their paper projects do rather require model inhabitants who are well-balanced, adaptable and identical, resembling those found in the yellow, ragged pages of More's *Utopia*.

In addition to fantastic visions, literary and creative conceptions, ordinary architectural projects have to be submitted and building subsequently carried out. Their authors are also expected to guarantee that their modern cities will solve the housing question, promote healthier living, prevent illnesses, make for a more cultured environment, solve traffic congestion and even remove dirt and dust from the streets.

Projects, models and drawings of future cities usually record only the completed, unchangeable appearance of streets, houses and town quarters. This is an ideal condition which can rarely, if ever, reflect all aspects of town life. In fact, other groups of people, such as doctors, politicians, economists, businessmen, social workers, council employees, small traders, builders and craftsmen, might be better suited to decide these aspects than urban planners themselves.

The building and construction of a human settlement is accompanied by various events. Let us imagine, looking at projects, how people and objects change in time and grow old, how some parts of the city lose their respective roles and acquire others for whatever reason.

Looking beyond the horiz-

on may not always be the best idea because it can lead to idealized conceptions of future settlements, devoid of any links with the real life of the town. It might disrupt town dwellers' personal links to the places which they comprehend and use daily.

At first sight these might seem unimportant details but the proper functioning of a settlement is dependent on them. We do not always realize how important it is for urban architecture to be varied and human in scale. This helps to differentiate the roles of individual city areas as it gives them their unique character and provides them with a history. This feature is called the 'memory' of cities.

The experience gathered during the construction of late 20th century cities, which has not always been for the best, somehow influences our ap-

By comparing old and new street plans and maps it is possible to follow the histories of towns and cities, from their origins to the present day, as if on a film. The evolution, on the one hand, of whole districts and, on the other, of individual city blocks can be traced. The evolving needs of a city's inhabitants, or the rise or decline of a city's major source of employment, can lead to radical changes over just a few years.

proach to them. Modern cities of past decades have often become a caricature of their 'Radiant Utopias'.

When looking at towns we are worried about polluting the environment and exhausting supplies of energy and foodstuffs on Earth. However, subconsciously we retain unlimited faith in modern technology, which might—perhaps—overcome all obstacles. The knowledge gathered by many sciences, including medicine and biology, also gives a hope of unveiling the mysterious processes which take place in the living organism of the city, such as complex interpersonal links and how a man perceives and responds to his urban surroundings. Thus, before we step out of the 20th century city gate, we have to try repeatedly to adapt this city to the changing needs, feelings and capabilities of its inhabitants. This is not a revolutionary finding, it has been voiced many times, but it still remains largely ignored and disregarded.

Without their inhabitants and their lives, cities would change into dusty museums for tourists, sad clusters of buildings which did not relate to each other, or ultimately

end up as archaeological sites if life ends there for whatever reasons. Thus, at the very end of this book, we would return to the beginning of the story of cities.

Cities and Their Crests

AMSTERDAM — the capital city of the Netherlands, also its largest city. It is situated at the mouth of the River Amstel. It has developed from an original fishing settlement. Since the 16th century Amsterdam has been one of the most important European cultural and trading centres. Its favourable location contributes greatly to its significance; it is still the most important Dutch port. It has 700,000 inhabitants, or about 1.5 million if we include its extensive suburbs. Amsterdam has preserved its unique appearance thanks to a network of canals (grachten), which are spanned by over 400 bridges. These canals delineate the fundamental structure of the city centre with its typical façades of residential houses built on wooden pillars embedded into the muddy canal botom.

ATHENS (Gk. Athinai) — the capital of Greece situated on the plain of Attica near the Aegean Sea. It is dominated by the Acropolis, formerly a fortified castle around which a settlement grew from the 2nd millennium B.C. According to legend, King Theseus joined the scattered settlements around the Acropolis into one city named after the Goddess Athene. Athens enjoyed political, cultural and economic ascendancy from the 6th century B.C.; the Acropolis was decorated with new temples. In 86 B.C., the Romans conquered the city. Its decline began in the 3rd century A.D. At present, Athens is the cultural, political and industrial centre of Greece. Its population, including the suburbs, is over 3 million.

BERLIN — was established in 1307 at the confluence of the Rivers Spree and Havel by the merger of two fishing settlements which were situated on sandy heath-lands. In accordance with the 1945 post-war Potsdam Conference, Berlin was divided into four occupied zones. West Berlin was created from the American, British and French zones. The Soviet zone became East Berlin, which was the capital of East Germany from 1949 to 1990 when East and West Germany re-unified. Berlin's post-war reconstruction was, however, marked by the construction of the Berlin Wall, which was finally demolished shortly before Germany's re-unification. Berlin has almost 3.5 million inhabitants.

BERN — the capital of Switzerland. According to legend it was founded by Duke Berchtold V in 1191. The historical centre is situated on the Aare River peninsula and has a regular layout. Numerous bridges connect the centre with residential and industrial quarters located beyond the river. Bern is an attractive city, which has many historical monuments and picturesque surroundings. The city itself has about 130,000 inhabitants whereas over 300,000 people live in the Bern conglomeration.

BRASILIA — the new capital of Brazil (the Federative Republic of Brazil) since 1960. It was built on a mountain plateau according to a winning design by L. Costa, the Brazilian architect and urban planner. This city was built 940 kilometres from the former Brazilian capital, Rio de Janeiro. It is an example of a well-planned city with outstanding modern buildings by O. Niemeyer, but has no particular history of its own and lacks a human feel. Brasilia has about 1.8 million inhabitants, many of whom are civil servants. It seem to be overshadowed by its much larger rivals — Rio de Janeiro with more than six million inhabitants and São Paulo with more than eleven million inhabitants. These two cities have poor living conditions but the country's social and economic life is concentrated there.

BRUSSELS (Fr. Bruxelles) — the capital of Belgium. The first written records date from the 8th century and refer to it as a settlement amidst the swamps of the River Rhine. Its name is derived from the Flemish 'brock' (= swamp) and 'sela' (= settlement). It is situated on the River Senne which is built over in the city centre. Brussels has wide streets and imposing squares with a lively metropolitan atmosphere. It is the headquarters of the EC and one of the most important commercial, social and cultural centres in Europe. It has over 1.3 million inhabitants, including the suburbs.

BUCHAREST (Romanian Bucureşti) — capital city of Romania. It is situated in the fertile Walachian plain of the River Dimbovita. Bucharest was probably already established in the 14th century. After 1861 when Bucharest became the capital of Romania, its imposing centre with wide boulevards and numerous parks was built, inspired by French urban planning. Low-rise buildings, however, predominate because of frequent earthquakes. Bucharest is the most important industrial and cultural centre of Romania and has about 1.1 million inhabitants.

BUDAPEST — the capital of Hungary. It was established in 1872 by the merger of Buda on the right bank of the Danube and Pest on the left bank. Budapest has grown on the site where Aquincum, one of the earliest central European settlements, stood. Aquincum, the centre of the Roman province of Panonia, was famous for its thermal springs, which have been in use ever since. Budapest enjoyed a large expansion in the last quarter of the 19th century when it acquired its metropolitan atmosphere. The buildings from that time have given Budapest its typical panoramic appearance. It has over 2 million inhabitants.

COPENHAGEN (Danish Kobenhavn) — the capital city of Denmark on Sjaelland Island. The first mention of Copenhagen refers to it as a fishing village called Havn (harbour) with a busy marketplace dating from the 11th cen-

tury. In the 12th century a fortification was built, which was soon surrounded by a town settlement. At present in addition to being the economic and cultural centre of Denmark, Copenhagen is the largest Danish commercial and military port. It has over 1.3 million inhabitants, including the suburbs. The city, which covers just one per cent of Denmark's territory, houses nearly one quarter of its population.

DELHI — the capital of India. Its significance as an important capital city dates from the early 13th century when the Delhi sultanate was established. The greatest building activity took place during the Mogul Empire — some important monuments from that era have been preserved to the present day. From 1911 to 1947 Delhi was the administrative centre of British India. New Delhi, originally planned as a governmental quarter, was built next to it and has become the centre of the modern city. Delhi, including the suburbs, has over 8.3 million inhabitants. Its population has been growing rapidly, as in other Indian cities (**Bombay** has more than eight million inhabitants while **Calcutta** has 9 million inhabitants).

HAMBURG — one of the free Hanseatic towns. It is a very important port on the lower reaches of the River Elbe, 110 km upstream from the North Sea. The Elbe is a tidal river which makes Hamburg accessible to even the largest ocean-going vessels. Thus, the city became an important port and industrial centre, which processed imported raw materials. Hamburg was established in the 8th century as a fortification guarding the confluence of the Rivers Elbe and Alster. It is also an important cultural centre with scientific institutes and a university. Its old town has an attractive historical centre. Hamburg has over 1.6 million inhabitants.

HELSINKI (Finnish Helsinky, Swedish Helsingfors) — the capital city of Finland since 1812. It is an important port on the Gulf of Finland. The city was established in the 16th century by Swedish King Gustavus I. After the great fire of 1808, Helsinki was reconstructed in the Classical style. In the 20th century it has become famous for the harmonious blending of new buildings with its surrounding countryside. This is true especially of the satellite settlements built since the 1960s, the most important of which is Tapiola. Helsinki itself has about 500,000 inhabitants but the Helsinki conglomeration has nearly one million inhabitants.

LISBON (Portuguese Lisboa) — the capital city of Portugal. It is a major port at the mouth of the River Tagus, on the Atlantic coast. In the 1st century B.C. a Roman military camp stood on the site and Lisbon was mentioned as a town at the beginning of the present millennium. Its significance resulted from its favourable siting for maritime voyages to Africa and South America. In addition, in the 20th century Lisbon has become an important crossroads of transatlantic air travel. Lisbon and its surroundings, like the majority of large cities, cluster together in an urban conglomeration which has over 1.6 million inhabitants.

century when a Moorish fortification stood there. After the Spanish victory over the Moors, a rich and prosperous town developed. It became the capital of Spain in 1561. Its later development was greatly influenced by the introduction of railways in the second half of the 19th century when Madrid became the transport, commercial and industrial centre of Spain. In the 20th century Madrid has grown into a modern metropolis with about 3 million inhabitants.

LONDON — the capital city of the United Kingdom, situated in the south-east of England. Already at the beginning of the millennium an enclosed settlement or town with a harbour stood on the River Thames. The Romans called it Londinium. From the 16th century London grew into the largest English port and a world famous commercial and industrial centre. It was reconstructed after the Great Fire of 1666. The peak of building activity came in the 18th and 19th centuries in the medieval City of London, when London became the world's largest metropolis. London has about 6.8 million inhabitants.

MADRID — the capital city of Spain situated in its centre on the River Manzanares. The first mention of Madrid dates from the 10th

MEXICO CITY (Spanish Ciudad de México) — the capital city of Mexico which rose from the site of the Aztec city of Tenochtitlan (founded c. 1325). Its centre is a mixture of buildings in various styles from Aztec culture to Spanish colonial architecture, 19th century pseudo-historical buildings to modern 20th century architecture. It is one of the fastest growing cities in the world and has about 9 million inhabitants or nearly 20 million if the suburban sprawl of temporary sheds and huts is included.

NAIROBI — the capital city of Kenya. It was founded in 1899 during the construction of the important railway link from Mombasa, an East African port. In the 1920s Nairobi was reconstructed as a modern city in a planned manner. At present it is among the most important of the African metropolises. It has over 1.1 million inhabitants. In addition, Nairobi is the seat of the United Nations Environment Programme and also of the United Nations Centre for Human Settlement — Habitat. The later organization's function is closely linked to the subject matter of this volume, i.e. issues of human settlements in the world.

MONTREAL — the largest Canadian city and port at the confluence of the Ottawa and the St. Lawrence Rivers. It was founded in 1642 on the site of a former Indian settlement. Montreal, which has over 3 million inhabitants, is the most important industrial and commercial centre in Canada. However, the much smaller city of **Ottawa**, situated on the river of the same name, with about 300,000 inhabitants, is the capital of Canada and the seat of administration and government.

MOSCOW (Russian Moskva) — the capital city of Russia and formerly of the Soviet Union. It is the political, cultural, industrial and transport centre of Russia, situated on the River Moskva. The first mention of the city dates from 1147. It has been the metropolis of a centralized Russia since the second half of the 15th century. In March 1918, the Soviet Government was transferred from Petrograd (St. Petersburg) to Moscow. Moscow has changed and grown much since then. It has over 8.8 million inhabitants.

NEW YORK — the largest city of the United States of America. It is full of contradictions and one of the world's most exciting cities. It was founded as New Amsterdam by Dutch settlers in 1624. Forty years later it was occupied by the English, who renamed it New York. From the beginning of the 19th century Manhattan Island at the mouth of the Hudson and the East River experienced large-scale construction activity, which led to a shortage of land and a subsequent steep rise in land prices. This contributed to the appearance of its archetypal panorama of concentrated high-rise buildings — skyscrapers. In addition to Manhattan, the other city boroughs are the Bronx, Brooklyn, Queens and Staten Island, which developed from the end of the 19th century. At present New York has over 7.3 million inhabitants. The population of the New York conglomeration reaches nearly twenty million as the urbanized area covers several districts of the states of New York and neighbouring New Jersey.

OSLO (formerly Christiania) — the capital city of Norway on the fjord of the same name. It is surrounded by wooded hills which create a spectacular panorama for the city. It was established in 1048 by the Viking King Harald III. After the fire of 1624 Oslo was re-founded by the King Christian IV and called Christiania in his honour. The name Oslo was used for an older southern part of the city but since 1925 the entire city has been known as Oslo. It is the most important Norwegian port and a crossroads which has until today preserved its unique role of being the entry gate to Norway. Oslo has about 500,000 inhabitants, with suburbs over 730,000.

PARIS — the capital city of France in the midst of the fertile Parisian plain. It stands on the site of an ancient oppidum built by the Gallic tribe of Parisii on the River Seine. The Romans called it Lutetia Parisiorum, which might be translated as 'the water stronghold of the Parisii'. From the 4th century the name became simplified and finally took its present form. Paris lies at the crossroads of important trade routes, and over the centuries its significance increased because of its harbour. It became an imposing and grandiose metropolis under the Prefect Haussmann from the 1850s. However, it had already enjoyed significant cultural and social changes and great construction activity in the 17th and 18th cen-

turies. Despite the fact that Paris in the 20th century has lost its unique position as the most modern European metropolis, it has remained a popular destination for tourists from all over the world. In the 1970s and 1980s new satellite towns were built in the suburbs of Paris, which successfully demonstrate the shift of emphasis in modern urban theories. Paris has about 2.3 million inhabitants within its historical boundaries while more than 8.5 million inhabitants live in Greater Paris.

PRAGUE (Czech Praha) — the capital of the Czech Republic. It is situated on the hilly terrain of the Prague valley through which flows the River Vltava. The name Praha originally referred to a stronghold established by the Přemyslid rulers on the left bank of the Vltava in the late 9th century A.D. Later, this name was adopted for the entire conglomeration in the Vltava valley, which consisted of dozens of settlements and homesteads. In the following centuries these gradually merged into a built-up urban area where firstly independent Prague towns were established, such as Staré Město (the Old Town), Malá Strana (the Little Quarter), Nové Město (the New Town), Hradčany (including the Castle). These independent towns were later unified into one city. At present Prague has a population of nearly 1.3 million.

ROME (Italian Roma) — the capital city of Italy on the River Tiber, about 25 kilometres from the sea. According to legend, the city was founded by the twin brothers Romulus and Remus in 753 B.C. However, the city is much older: it was created from Latini and Sabine settlements which had already existed in the 10th and 9th centuries B.C. From the 3rd century B.C., Rome was the richest and the greatest city of the ancient world. Its decline started in the 4th century A.D. when the Roman Empire was divided into its Eastern and Western parts, culminating in the fall of the Western Roman Empire in A.D. 476 when Rome was ransacked by barbarian tribes. It flourished again with the arrival of High Renaissance and Baroque styles in the 16th century when Rome became the centre of Christendom. Rome is now a modern metropolis. In addition to being highly industrialized, Rome is an important crossroads and a social and cultural centre very popular with tourists. It has over 2.8 million inhabitants.

SOFIA (Bulgarian Sofiya) — the capital city of Bulgaria. It is situated in the centre of the Balkan Peninsula, in a fertile valley in the foothills of the Vitocha mountains. The city was founded by the Romans near a Thracian settlement and called after the local tribe Serdica Ulpia. It was the capital of the province of Dacia under the Emperor Diocletian. Its later fortunes were mixed and it was often renamed: Sredec in the Middle Ages, Triadica and finally, in the 14th century, Sofiya after the patron saint of a cathedral which is one of the most outstanding and most admired historical buildings in the present-day city. Modern Sofia is the political and cultural centre of Bulgaria and its major industrial town. With suburbs, it has over 1.2 million inhabitants.

STOCKHOLM — the capital city of Sweden at the outlet of Lake Malar, on the Baltic Sea. It is called the 'Queen of the Baltic' for the beauty of its surroundings: the built-up areas spread to picturesque coastlines of peninsulas and islands, rocky hills and the plain. The city is divided into smaller settlements which have good communication links with the cen-

(the biggest were in 1703 and 1923). This is reflected in the construction technology: in addition to earthquake-resistant high-rise buildings there are endless districts of low-rise family houses built from light building materials, particularly wood. These account for the relatively densely built-up appearance of the conglomeration. Therefore, statistics on Tokyo's population vary greatly. The region directly administered by the local authorities has about 8.3 million inhabitants, with suburbs about 12 million, but in reality ribbon development near Tokyo and Yokohama embraces many other smaller towns and has over 20 million inhabitants.

tre. This site was already inhabited in the 12th century. In 1255 an island settlement was fortified and became the centre of a town, which soon became an important international trade crossroads, with a major harbour and dock area, later with manufacturing industries as well. Stockholm is a pleasant and well-ordered city with over 600,000 inhabitants. Greater Stockholm has about 1.5 million inhabitants.

TOKYO — the capital city of Japan. It is situated at the head of Tokyo Bay. It was established in the 12th century as Yeddo. In 1868 it became the capital city and was renamed Tokyo. It suffers from frequent earthquakes

VIENNA (German Wien) — the capital of Austria. It is conveniently situated on the River Danube. The Romans established a military camp Vindobona on the site of a Celtic settlement (from the Celtic 'windo' = white). A busy marketplace around the camp later developed into a town. When Vienna's fortified walls were pulled down in 1857 and a planned reconstruction started, this marked a milestone in the transformation of Vienna to a modern metropolis. These urban changes have greatly enhanced present-day Vienna's atmosphere. Vienna has over 1.5 million inhabitants, with suburbs about 2 million.

WARSAW (Polish Warszawa) — the capital city of Poland since the 16th century. It was established on the River Vistula in the 13th century. It was devastated in World War II — eighty per cent of its buildings were razed to the ground and more than 800,000 inhabitants were killed, most of them in the Jewish Ghetto. Soon after liberation, the re-building and construction of the historical centre began, largely based on Canaletto's paintings. Warsaw has quickly grown into the largest industrial, cultural and political centre of Poland. In 1945, one month after liberation, Warsaw had 160,000 inhabitants. Thirty five years later its population has grown to over 1.6 million inhabitants.

WASHINGTON, D.C. — the capital city of the United States of America. In 1791 the American Congress agreed to the establishment of the new Federal Capital. P. Ch. L'Enfant, a French military engineer, designed the city, which accounts for its Classical urban style, inspired by the grandiose plans of Paris. The atmosphere and the life of the city is largely determined by the presence of Government bodies, universities and scientific institutes. Washington has about 600,000 inhabitants, the whole 'urban agglomeration' has a population of more than 3.9 million.

Select Bibliography

BENEVELO, Leonardo, *The History of the City*, Scholar Press, London; MIT Press, Cambridge, Mass., 1980

FISHMAN, Robert, *Urban Utopias in the Twentieth Century*, MIT Press, Cambridge, Mass., 1982

GOSLING, David, and MAITLAND, Barry, *Concepts of Urban Design*, Academy Editions, London, 1984

HALL, Peter, *Cities of Tomorrow*, Basil Blackwell, Oxford, 1988

JACOBS, Jane, *The Death and Life of Great American Cities*, Penguin Books, Harmondsworth, 1965 (first published U.S.A. 1961)

JENCKS, Charles, *Modern Movements in Architecture*, 2nd edition, Penguin Books, Harmondsworth, 1985

KRIER, Leon, *Houses, Palaces, Cities*, Architectural Design Profile, Academy Editions, London, 1984

KRIER, Rob, *Urban Space*, Academy Editions, London, 1979

MUMFORD, Lewis, *The City in History*, A Harvest/HBJ Book, New York, 1961

MUMFORD, Lewis, *The Urban Prospect*, A Harvest/HBJ Book, New York, 1968

MUMFORD, Lewis, *The Myth of the Machine*, vols. I, II, A Harvest/HBJ Book, New York, 1967, 1970

NORBERG-SCHULZ, Christian, *Genius Loci*, Academy Editions, London, 1980

ROSSI, Aldo, *The Architecture of the City*, Oppositions Books, MIT Press, Cambridge, Mass., 1985 (first published 1966)

SITTE, Camillo, *The Art of Building Cities*, Reinhold Publishing Corp., New York, 1945

VITRUVIUS, *Ten Books on Architecture*, translated by M. H. Morgan, Dover Publications Inc., New York, 1960

VENTURI, Robert, SCOTT-BROWN, Denise, and IZENOUR, Steven, *Learning from Las Vegas*, MIT Press, Cambridge, Mass. 1977

WARD, Stephen V., *The Garden City: Past, Present and Future*, E. & F. N. Spon., London, 1992

Index

Figures in italics refer to illustrations, maps and tables